Common Birds of Atlanta

by

Jim Wilson
&
Anselm Atkins

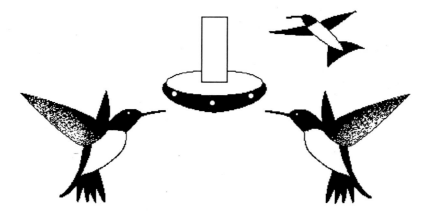

ACKNOWLEDGEMENTS

The authors are grateful for the help that they received from many sources. The photographer thanks all of the many people who allowed him to set up and photograph birds in their backyards, including Eileen Breding, Leslie Curran, Ann Brodie Hill, Earl Horn, Karen Pralinsky, Rusty Trump, Thad and Robin Weed, Victor Williams, and Linda Wilson. In particular, Melanie Haire, Frank McCamey, Monteen McCord, and the Chattachoochee Nature Center were invaluable as resources, and he greatly appreciated the advice and help of Frank Kiernan, Chang-Kwei Lin, and Jean Torbit at Emory University. We also thank Georgann Schmalz, Barbara Gray, Jeff Sewell, and Giff Beaton for checking the photographs and text for errors as we proceeded. Any errors in the final version, however, are the authors' responsibility. Some of the computer graphics and descriptions appeared previously in slightly different form in *Wingbars*, the monthly newsletter of the Atlanta Audubon Society.

Our great appreciation goes to our wives, Kay Wilson and Margaret Kavanaugh, who tolerated us during the years of producing this book.

5th Edition, 2005

Photographs and cover design by Jim Wilson
Text and computer graphics © *Birdgrafx* by Anselm Atkins

To all the people who love birds
and seek to protect them

Printed in Korea

Common Birds of Atlanta
arranged by size

INTRODUCTION

How to Use this Book

"What bird is that in my yard?" If you live in Atlanta or anywhere else in the Piedmont region, you can probably answer that question by looking through this book. We have chosen sixty-one of the most common birds, the ones you'd be most likely to see, and provided you with the means of making a quick identification.

Our photographs can easily be matched with the bird you are watching. Along with the photograph will be a brief, informative text telling you what to observe as you watch your bird, along with other notable facts about the species.

The birds in the book are arranged by size, starting with the tiny ruby-throated hummingbird and ending with the great blue heron. The blue jay and northern cardinal are somewhere near the middle. With size as your guide, you won't waste time searching the wrong part of the book. The number of a bird on the list corresponds with its page number. The sizes given are the measurements of live birds and thus are a little smaller than numbers based on dead, relaxed specimens.

Many of the birds of our area are only migrants. They don't live here year-round. We have excluded these, except for a few very noticeable ones such as the brightly colored indigo bunting and the white-throated sparrow (a common winter ground-feeder). There are also certain other birds, although they live here all the time, that are not frequently encountered. The loggerhead shrike is an example. These uncommon birds are omitted.

Start with the color photographs. These have been taken with an eye to presenting aspects of the bird that are most important in identification. With the Carolina wren, for example, it was necessary to have a picture that showed the white eye-stripe, the buffy breast, and the typically upturned tail. If the male and female of a species are markedly different (as they are in the northern cardinal), care has been taken to show both sexes. At times two views of a bird were necessary to show various other features. It was not our intention to produce great shots with beautiful vistas or dramatic poses, and many of our subjects were near backyard feeders just like yours. Our degree of success is measured, rather, by our ability to show you the prominent "field marks" and colors which you will need for identifying your birds.

The text tells you mainly what the bird is supposed to look like, as a supplement to the photograph. Something is said of its song, because although birds don't sing all the time, their song is an important identifying feature if you happen to hear it. Mention is made of the bird's preferred habitat: in swamps, thickets, open fields, high in conifers, etc., for birds don't live just anywhere. Each species has its typical place of residence. Its usual food, moreover, will often be given, as well as its nesting habits and other interesting facts.

Birds: An Appreciation

Since the dawn of time humans have noticed birds and taken delight in them. Our art and literature make regular reference to them, and science (ornithology) studies them exhaustively. While we may not "love" birds the way we sometimes do our mammalian pets, our admiration for them is boundless.

Birds are many things to us. They embody wildness, yet they are numerous, easy to see, and frequently tolerant of human presence. Their ability to fly stirs deep yearnings in us, making birds the subject of art, myth, and religion. We appreciate their beautiful colors and shapes as much as they themselves do. We enjoy their song, simple or complex as it may be. We can be endlessly entertained -- if we are observant -- by the intricacies of their behavior. Nor can we fail to be impressed by their sheer variety. And though the days of skies being "blackened with birds" may unfortunately be over, there are still times when their sheer number is impressive. Who in our region has not seen the seemingly endless waves of blackbirds in the evening skies as they wing home to roost?

There are people, indeed, who might well be called "bird crazy." Who knows but what the authors themselves could be numbered among these? Don't worry: this disease cannot be communicated through books. But beware the birds themselves! Watching them, feeding them, and identifying them may start you on the slippery path of no return. Next you'll be buying binoculars and signing up for field trips with your local Audubon Society. After that there's no telling. Bird watching is indeed a hobby for a lifetime, admitting innumerable levels of interest, commitment, and reward.

Birds in Peril

Yet all is not well in the avian world. Humans are hard, vigorous users of the world and its resources. What we do is not without its effect on other plants and animals. Fact is, our activities are causing the decline or disappearance of many other species. It's not that we wish harm to the co-inhabitants of our planet. It's just that very often we need or want what they have -- and so we take it. Usually what we take is the habitat in which other species live. And indeed our appetite for the habitats of plants and other animals has been ravenous. The decline in duck populations, for example, is not due to evil duck hunters. It is due, rather, to decent, law-abiding farmers who simply want to plow their wetlands under so we humans can have more food to eat. All it takes to wipe out ducks is having more human mouths to feed. Unless we can devise ways of not taking the animals' space away from them, they will, species by species, go the way of the dodo.

The abundance of birds -- or their scarcity -- tells us how humans are affecting bird, plant, and animal habitats. Results are what you'd expect. As the equatorial rain forests of the world are leveled at a galloping rate, the migratory birds that winter there dwindle. As wooded nesting areas in North America are used for human development, so do these same birds dwindle all the more. It's a documented fact. And people who love birds worry about it.

People who love humanity worry about it, too, because birds are an indicator of the general health of our environment as a whole. Remember when bald eagles and ospreys and peregrine falcons were disappearing because widespread use of DDT was causing their eggs to crush and fail? The birds were, by their own deaths, telling us that too many harmful chemicals were loose in our land. Such chemicals eventually work their harm on humans, too. Today we are all concerned about the indiscriminate release of various chemicals into our surroundings. Like the miner's canary, our everyday backyard birds can, by their disappearance, often give the first warning sign of something gone awry with our own human habitat.

It is for this reason that your local Audubon Society not only encourages your interest in birds, but also reminds you that good conservation habits are essential if we are to continue to live in a world friendly to both birds and humans.

The Next Step To Enjoying Birds

There are many ways bird watchers can enrich their experience with birds. You who own this book already know the thrill of watching and identifying the common birds in your everyday surroundings. What else can you do to increase that enjoyment?

Equipment. Binoculars are indispensable for most bird identification. Start with a cheap pair of 7 X 35 binoculars. By the time you want something better, you will know what to buy. As you grow more experienced you may want a more complete field guide (see our list below). To go with your field guides, you may want to obtain some tapes or CDs of bird songs. Much of your experience with birds will probably be by listening alone.

Websites. There are several good websites and discussion groups that cover items related to our birds. The Atlanta Audubon Society's site is www.atlantaaudubon.org, and the Georgia Ornithological Society site is: www.gos.org. Georgia Birders Online (GABO) is an email group that can be reached at GABO-L@listserv.uga.edu and allows everyone to discuss birds and find out where to go for many species. There are also hotlines that can be called for the Rare Bird Alerts (Georgia Rare Bird Alert: 770-493-8862). Further, many of the Audubon chapters in Georgia have their own websites that you can find out more on local activities. Go first to the National Audubon website (www.nas.org) and then to the local ones from there.

Field Trips. Audubon chapters sponsor many group bird walks to see both resident and migratory birds, common and rare. *Common Birds of Atlanta* does not cover all migrants, but by taking advantage of these free field trips, you can observe and learn hundreds of species of birds.

Christmas Bird Count. Every December, the Audubon Chapters in the state sponsor holiday bird counts. On this day, you drive into the countryside with several other bird lovers, one of who is your guide. You spend the day identifying and recording every single bird you see or hear. The atmosphere is fun and casual, but the results are sent in to a national headquarters for the data. Through the efforts of CBC volunteers, it has been possible to compile nationwide statistics on the health or decline of all of our species. To participate in a CBC, contact your nearest Audubon chapter.

FeederWatch. For the past decade, Cornell University has sponsored a nationwide bird count that lets backyard bird watchers like you make a small contribution to bird research. From November through March, the observer sets aside two days every other week during which he or she spends whatever time is convenient to observe the birds at their feeder. They also conduct a watch day for migratory birds in May and a Great Backyard Bird Count in February (http://birdsource.org/GBBC/). To sign up, contact Cornell Lab of Ornithology, 159 Sapsucker Woods Rd., Ithaca NY 14850, or check http://birds.cornell.edu.

Birdathon. Every year, many Audubon Society chapters sponsor a birdathon as a money-raising event. Birders find sponsors (often at the workplace) who will donate so much per bird species seen by you. All you have to do then is go have a wonderful day birding – and Audubon makes money to conserve our birds!

Checklists. A checklist is a list of all the birds that have been observed in a designated place – perhaps in the state, city, refuge, or nature center. The list tells you not only what species might be seen, but what times of year each species occurs and in what numbers (common, rare, etc.). It may tell you whether they nest there, also.

Listing. It may occur to you to want to keep your personal list of all the birds that you have identified over the years. First is your lifelist – all the species you have seen wherever you have been. There are over 700 species of birds to be seen in the U.S. alone, and about 10,000 in the world. Next is your yardlist – species seen or heard in your own yard, which could be well over 100 species! Some enthusiastic birders keep other lists, such as state or even county lists.

Other Good Bird Books

As your interest in birds increases, you will want to consult more detailed guides to bird identification ("field guides"), as well as general introductions to the study of birds. We list a few of the best.

Erlich, Paul, Dobkin, David, and Wheye, Darryl. *The Birder's Handbook: A Field Guide to the Natural History of North American Birds.* Simon and Schuster, Inc.: New York, 1988. This comprehensive handbook is suitable for advanced birders.

Pasquier, Roger F. *Watching Birds: An Introduction to Ornithology.* Houghton Mifflin Company: Boston, 1980. Pasquier's is a good general introduction to the subject.

Peterson, Roger Tory. *A Field Guide to the Birds of Eastern and Central North America.* Houghton Mifflin Company: Boston, 1980. Peterson developed the very useful method of noting "field marks," the special features that make identification quick and certain. The range maps, unfortunately, are not on the same page as the drawings. Lifelike paintings by Peterson. Recommended for beginning and intermediate birders.

Robbins, Chandler S., Bruun, Bertel, and Zim, Herbert S. *Birds of North America.* Golden Press: New York, 1966. Pictures and maps are together, and sonograms or "voice pictures" are included. The "field mark" method, however, is not used.

Sibley, David Allen. *The Sibley Guide to Bird*s. Chanticleer Press, Inc.: New York, 2000. Too large for use as a field guide, but excellent for showing various subtleties of each species. Smaller, more select versions available.

Stokes, Donald and Lillian. *Stokes Field Guide to Birds: Eastern Region.* Boston: Little, Brown and Company, 1996. Excellent photographs showing different plumages and most field marks. All information is on one page, including up-to-date range map, behavior, and conservation status.

RUBY-THROATED HUMMINGBIRD
Archilochus colubris
3"

In the eastern United States, the hummingbird we're most likely to see is the ruby-throated, and then only in summer. In recent years, however, more and more sightings of western hummers have been reported. These are winter birds, present when ruby-throats have migrated south. Our summer hummingbirds are all ruby-throats.

A male hummingbird's throat-feathers are called his "gorget." Our hummer's is red, with black chin above. The back is green, underparts white-gray. Females and juveniles lack the throat patch. Since the red on the patch is iridescent, it may appear black in different lighting conditions. An immature ruby male shows a speckled throat.

They are very possessive of their food sources, which are critical for survival. At the feeder you will see them chasing each other away, and hear their squeaky, twittery chatter. Otherwise they just hum (with their rapid wing beats). Hummingbirds can assume many acrobatic positions and even fly backwards.

Hummers sip nectar with tubular tongues out of long-necked flowers, preferring red and orange colors. They also take spiders and insects and rob sap from sapsucker holes. Because of their high metabolism and extremely rapid wing beats, hummers need to feed nearly all the time. At night, to save energy, they may fall into a deep torpor something like hibernation.

Fill your home feeder with four parts water to one part sugar. Boil briefly. Change the fluid at least weekly and cleanse the feeder. Do not add red coloring, just have something red on or near the feeder itself. Female hummingbirds make a tiny nest and feed their young by regurgitation, sticking their long bills right down into the chick's gullet.

Photos: The bright red gorget of the male (upper right) becomes completely black when the light comes from a different angle (upper left). The female has a white throat and white-tipped outer tail feathers (lower).

BROWN-HEADED NUTHATCH
Sitta pusilla
3 ½"

High in the pines you hear a squeaking noise. It sounds like the squeaky toy in your kid's bathtub. You look up and see two or three very small birds skittering around in the pine fronds and cones. They dart actively from place to place. At that height and against the light of the sky they look simply dark. You can just make out that they have practically no tails. Put those four things together: small size, squeaky toy, pine trees, short tail and the mystery is solved. They're brown-headed nuthatches.

Viewed up close this nuthatch is a handsome little bird. It really does have a rusty brown cap and nape. Cheek and underparts are white, back and wings gray. It is even smaller than your very common chickadee, so you will have a difficult time checking out its characteristics unless you entice it close with food.

You may occasionally glimpse one at your feeding station. They grab a sunflower seed and fly away quickly. Up in the pines they're eating the pine seeds, along with any insects they come across.

For a nest the nuthatch hollows a hole in a dead pine, often a rather small one. The family forages together for a while in the company of other small birds. They like black-oiled sunflower seeds.

Our nuthatch is confined to the Southeast, where it can be found throughout the year at lower elevations. But now here's an interesting thing. Out west it has a counterpart, the pygmy nuthatch, which is much like ours except for its gray-brown cap and peeping song. Thus you can virtually see the speciation that has taken place. When the Great Plains were formed, the ancestral species perforce divided into two non-communicating populations, each of which then went its separate way: brown-headed here, pygmy there. Those vast, dry, treeless plains served as a divide for many other species, too.

Photos: The brown cap is clearly visible in both positions, as is the white breast. Note the dark gray back and comparatively short tail.

RUBY-CROWNED KINGLET
Regulus calendula
3 ¾"
GOLDEN-CROWNED KINGLET
Regulus satrapa
3 ½"

The **ruby-crowned kinglet** skitters quickly through the trees searching for insects, often in the company of other small birds. One thing about him makes him special: the flaming scarlet crest, which he usually raises only when he gets in a snit with rival males or when scolding a screech owl.

This kinglet has a light breast with olive-brown or gray wings and back. Its white eye-ring is conspicuous and separates it from the golden-crowned. Its highly visible white wingbars also contrast with the dull bars of the latter. In the field, look for eye-ring and wingbar. Additional marks are a short tail and constant wing-flicking. Don't expect to see the crest.

On his wintering grounds in the South you may hear him scold, and think at first of titmouse or wren. His loud song, however, is one you'll not hear on a Christmas Bird Count.

The **golden-crowned kinglet** is similar to the ruby-crowned in looks and habits, but with some important differences. Notice first that the golden-crowned has no eye ring, just a solid black eye with a white stripe above it. Second, the golden-crowned kinglet's wingbars are not as distinct as those of its cousin. Third, we can usually see the gold stripe on the head (with orange center for the male) whereas often, with the ruby-crowned, no ruby is visible. The call heard in winter, when the bird is in our range, is a bell-like "tsee", usually given in threes.

Kinglets are very active, darting among the bare twigs of winter trees, or searching the green boughs of pine. Their food may be berries of honeysuckle and poison ivy, or whatever remains from the bounty of summer. They also like to flick their wings in and out while foraging.

Photos: (Above) Ruby-crowned with white eye-ring and white wingbar, and, for the right view, a raised red crest. (Below) Note the slight yellowish tint on the golden-crowned's wingbars. Clearly seen also are the dark eye, white eye-stripe, and yellow crown bordered with black (no orange showing).

3

CAROLINA CHICKADEE
Poecile carolinensis
4 ¼"

A very common small gray bird with a black cap, black bib, white cheeks, white belly, that's your chickadee. They'll come around your house if you have any trees at all. They'll be at your feeder in an instant if you put out sunflower seed. Watch how one eats. It will pick through the seeds, casting away ones it doesn't want, till it finds just the right one. Then it flies off with it to a nearby branch, holds the seed between its toes, and pecks at the husk. Soon it flies back for more.

When it's not eating birdseed, the chickadee searches foliage for insects, often hanging upside down from a twig to see what's underneath.

The chickadee sings its name, as many birds do: chick-a-dee-dee-dee, rather buzzily. In spring it gives a four-note up-and-down whistled song, which can be described as fee-bee-fee-bay. They also produce a high squeaking that is hard to describe.

The nest is a hollow dug from rotten wood; or it could be any similar cavity, found or provided. There are usually six eggs, white with reddish speckles. Both parents bring food.

Carolina chickadees like to hang around with their blood cousin, the tufted titmouse. Often you'll see a few of each at the same time. Chickadees will let you get fairly close. Seems like the larger the bird, the more wary it is. Perhaps the chickadee knows it's not big enough to make a mouthful.

Birds are not cute. Most would be described as awesome, majestic, pretty, handsome, interesting, weird, or maybe lackluster or pesky. But one bird can be described only as cute, and that bird is the chickadee. That's why it's on all the cards in gift shops. And that is why you can't stop loving the chickadee.

Photos: Note the striking white cheek, with jet black above and below. The bill is very tiny.

AMERICAN GOLDFINCH
Carduelis tristis
4 1/2"

There's good reason why the American goldfinch has often been called "wild canary." In his spring breeding plumage the male is bright lemon yellow with contrasting black wings, tail, and cap. The female's yellow is paler with a dull brown back.

In winter, both sexes are dull: brownish gray with just the barest blush of yellow, and a black not quite so stark. The wing will show one white stripe and a yellow epaulet.

Goldfinches are notorious for liking thistles, an expensive seed for feeders. They seem just as happy with sunflower seeds, however, and can be found regularly at the trough alongside other finches. Being a seed-eater, the goldfinch has a thick, stubby bill good for crushing seeds. Any yellow-colored warbler that looks a little like a goldfinch will have a delicate, pointed warbler's bill (warblers eat mainly insects).

The goldfinch in flight can often be identified by the undulations and the call that often accompanies it: "per-chik-o-ree." The song is long, high, and sweet.

Goldfinches may flock by the dozens or hundreds in trees with seeds, or in fields. So devoted is the goldfinch to thistles that it even makes its nest out of their down. Nesting seems to keep time with the maturation of thistles. Farmer, leave those pretty purple thistles in your pastures!

Around July of each year, the adults and fledglings may strike out farther from their thistle fields and come to your feeders, so make sure you have sunflower seed as well as some thistle seed out to accommodate them.

Photos: (Above) A summer male in full color: black cap and wings, white wingbars, the rest a very bright lemon yellow. (Below) A winter female who is essentially gray-brown with little yellow on her; a winter male might have a little yellow only at the shoulder and on the face and no black cap.

The names of birds make us aware of how varied and subtle the colors of nature are. To name a few of these: cerulean, lazuli, buff, bay, rose, ferruginous, rufous, ash, ruby, glaucous, chestnut, clay, and many more. Thus we come to the indigo bunting. The male indigo is truly a rare color.

City dwellers, unfortunately, will have to do a little driving to reach this bird's favored habitat, for it loves the open country. Even there it is present only from spring through fall.

The bunting feeds and nests in heavy undergrowth; hence you'll seldom discover it on the ground. No matter, the male sings from an exposed perch, frequently in plain view near the tip of a tree. You'll find it around the edge of a field, or on a small tree in the field. You can see them on wires and even on the rooftops of outbuildings.

The male's song is sweet and distinctive: something like "sweet-sweet, where-where, here-here, see it-see it." The paired notes are on different pitches, weakening and descending.

The female indigo bunting has brown wings, tan head, and buffy breast with a hint of brown striping. In fall and winter the male resembles his mate, except for touches of blue. The male always has a little black on his wings and tail. If you're able to view the indigo's beak, notice its finch-like thickness and its color: dark above, light below.

A similar, but more rare, bird that you'll see in the countryside is the blue grosbeak (not included here). It is a little larger, is a darker, duller blue, and has two reddish-brown wingbars.

Photos: (Above) Male all blue except for black touches on wing and tail. Note light lower mandible. (Below) The female has brown plumage, with wings darker than head. Some light streaking is visible on sides and upper breast.

CHIPPING SPARROW
Spizella passerina
4 ¾"

Like the field sparrow, the chipping sparrow has a light gray, unstreaked breast. What marks him best is his broad, chestnut cap. Look also for the black stripe through the eye and the white line just above it. In winter the bird is plainer: the rusty cap is replaced with a dull brown one.

The chippy's song is a rattle or trill, all on one note. It seems quieter, drier, and faster than the trill of the pine warbler, with whose song it might be confused. One may need practice to keep from getting the two songs mixed up. Both species are out there during our Christmas Bird Counts, and both are singing: same in spring and early summer.

Though chipping sparrows may come to a feeder, we usually see them in flocks out in the countryside. You can see hundreds feeding in the gray winter corn stubble, or hiding in a hedgerow, or feeding on the grass in the front yards of homes. Their flocks are typically larger than those of the field sparrow.

The chippy's conical bill marks it as a seed-crusher. That's what it's hunting in the fields. But of course it eats insects too. Most perching birds do feed their young insects, and these seed eaters are no different.

The Marietta area use to have the high count in the nation for chipping sparrows (thousands), but human developments have taken over their habitats and left little for these birds to feed and nest. This is true for many of our declining bird species with 85 species being on the Georgia Conservation Priority Bird Species list (see Important Bird Areas under Atlanta Audubon's website).

Photos: (Above) Perfect view of the reddish cap at its best; also note the black stripe through the eye and the white stripe above it. (Below) Would you confuse this winter plumage with that of the field sparrow? Gray breast is the same. But look: the bill is not orange-pink and the cheek has no brown: Chippy.

YELLOW-RUMPED WARBLER
Dendroica coronata
4 ¾"

The yellow-rumped warbler is especially interesting because it has two distinct forms, eastern and western, which can be defined as subspecies. Here you see evolution in the actual process of dividing one species into two. At present the two forms can still interbreed when they meet, so are lumped together. Given enough time, however, they could very well become two different kinds of warblers. Of course, this has already happened with our other forty or so species of warblers, which have come, by circuitous routes, from a single common ancestor.

Our eastern form was formerly called the "myrtle warbler," and the western form "Audubon's warbler," as if they already were two species until ornithologists noticed that they were still interbreeding where their range overlapped. A very similar cousin, the magnolia warbler, has already split apart and gone its own way.

The yellow-rumped is best noticed by just that: the yellowish splotch of feathers above its tail. Old-time birders lovingly call it the "butter-butt". It is a winter migrant present in Georgia only from Nov. through May, with a high concentration on the coast.

In winter plumage, the bird is drab and nondescript, though the yellow rump remains visible, as well as a tinge of yellow on the upper breast near the wing. But in spring breeding plumage, the male is really an eyeful. There's a black eye-patch and black on the breast, with yellow on the crown, and brighter yellow on that breast and rump. (The "Audubon's" plumage in the West sports a yellow throat, while the yellow-rumped's is white.)

The song is a trill with some fluctuation; the call, a "check" sound. The warbler feeds largely on insects, even taking them on the wing like a flycatcher. In winter it resorts to berries. It is often found in flocks in trees or high brush. At those times you can hear its constant little "check" call.

Photos: Male (above) acquiring spring breeding plumage: lots of black, some white, and bits of yellow. Below: a winter or female-plumaged bird, dull and brownish, but still with that yellow rump and a little yellow wash below the bend of the wing. Sexes are alike in winter.

CAROLINA WREN
Thyrothorus lodvicianus
4 ¾"

This little brown bird is among our most loveable. It is distinguished from other birds by its uptilted tail and from other wrens seen in Atlanta, such as the house wren and winter wren, by its prominent white eye-stripe and buffy breast. Larger than other eastern wrens, it is still less than five inches long. It ranges over the whole southeast.

The Carolina wren may bring leaves into your old hat hanging in the garage or to a nest in your hanging planter – one of its favorite places to raise a family. One once built a nest under the hood of a car! It accepts any protected place, and seems to like being near human habitation. Several broods are raised each year. You can often see a little band of four or five wrens noisily flitting through the brush around your yard.

The Carolina wren lives mainly on insects, often hunting low to the ground. It hops briskly over brush piles, tree stumps, and shrubs, searching every cranny. But it will also come to a feeder, where it prefers to eat alone. It seems to like food particles left behind by the other birds.

This wren has a most amazing repertoire of song, perhaps more than any other bird in the South, boasting at least 125 distinguishable songs. Its bright, cheery songs are much louder than the singer's size would suggest. The notes are in groups of threes or fours. You'll hear "teacher, teacher, teacher" or "tea-kettle, tea-kettle, tea-kettle." The wren will sing triplets of "twinkie," "courtesy," "piecemeal," "trilogy," or almost any word you want it to. Yet these aren't random sounds, they're particular songs. It also has a fussy hissing scold, a dry rattling "answering" trill, and a repeated bright rolling trill. Sometimes this wonderful little bird seems responsible for half the bird song in your yard.

Photos: (Above) Bill is long and wickedly curved, breast buff. (Below) Note the cocked tail and the strong white stripe above the eye. Male and female are alike.

PINE WARBLER
Dendroica pinus
4 ¾"

It's a dull winter day, you're looking at gray clouds behind a mask of green pines, and suddenly you see a bright spot of yellow. There's only one bird this happy little spot could turn into: the pine warbler.

Just to be sure, you check for some field marks: Two white wingbars and largish, for a warbler, with a stronger-looking beak than usual. Then you confirm: greenish-olive above, white toward the back of a yellow belly with a hint of a yellow eye-ring. It's the pine warbler! And just then he lets loose its trilling warble. That settles it.

Be aware, though, that not all pine warblers have a lot of yellow. Females are duller, immatures are duller, and even males can vary. But on your Christmas Count, even the faintest hint of yellow will be enough to give the pine warbler away.

Pine warblers are in our area year round. In the fall they can be fairly nondescript, but you can certainly pick them out in winter, when few other warblers are around, and in spring, when the males are in their best plumage. Though pine warblers may sometimes be spotted away from pines, they nest in pines 99% of the time, being one of the earliest to nest in the spring.

Do pine warblers ever come to winter bird feeders? Like other warblers, they feed almost exclusively on insects. As there are few insects in winter, they come to your feeder on rare occasions. But if you put out a suet feeder, you'll see them all the time.

Back to that trilling warble, or "musical trill, slower than a chipping sparrow's." You can learn to recognize this song. Just be aware that chippies, too, can sing from pine trees.

Photos: In both pictures, observe the two white wingbars and the split eye-ring with yellow to pale yellow below, gray to olive above. Note that the amount of yellow can vary considerably.

The field sparrow is a bird of the countryside. It prefers open areas with small trees, brushy pastures, and abandoned farmland. Unlike the migrant white-throat, it stays with us year-round; and, also unlike that bird, it seldom comes to city feeding stations. Sometimes in winter it feeds with other birds on the lawns of farm houses then scurries to the safety of an overhead tree. The flock leaves in parts: now some, now more, now even more, you never guessed there could be so many birds hidden there on the ground! They scurry to cover like leaves in a storm.

What food is it looking for? Seeds and small insects. Nesting is usually in thick briers. Young are said to be able to tumble out of the nest prematurely and make it on their own, hidden in the grass.

The field sparrow is recognized visually by several marks. The breast is very plain, a pale buff. Its conical, sparrow-shaped beak is described by many as "pinkish", but to most people it is seen more as a bright orange color, unlike that of any of its cousins. Cheeks and crown are streaked with gray and reddish brown. It has a white eye-ring and white wingbars.

In late spring and summer, the field sparrow's distinctive breeding song can be heard everywhere in the countryside, where fallow fields, brushy pastures, and grassy yards are its rightful place. Its song starts with a few bouncy whistles which grow faster and faster until they become a rising trill. Once you've heard this song you'll know it forever, and always rejoice in its beauty. Ah, there are field sparrows out there!

.

Photos: Here you see all the marks for identification: the pale, buffy breast, pink/orange beak, cheek striped with rust and gray, white wingbars, and white-eye ring.

RED-EYED VIREO
Vireo olivaceous
5"

The red-eyed vireo is one of a group of small, warbler-like birds. What best tells the groups apart is the bill: the typical vireo bill is longer and thicker than that of most warblers and has a little hook at the tip of the upper mandible.

Vireos are divided into two clans: those with wingbars and a white or black "mask" around the eye, and those with no bars or mask, but, instead, a white eye-stripe. The red-eye is in the latter category. Its white stripe is bordered thinly with black. With that mark goes a prominent gray cap. For the rest, look for dark olive or greenish back and wings, and white or light underparts. The red eye is not a field mark: it won't be noticeable unless you get a very close look in just the right light.

Like other vireos, the red-eyed vireo feeds almost exclusively on insects. It works its way slowly through the foliage, looking around carefully for the caterpillars of moths and butterflies, or any other crawly thing. It sees what it needs to see: birds have keen vision and see colors well.

This vireo gives a short, two-phrase song: maybe "chee-ay," short pause, "ee-yoo." It sings its composition over and over, with variations, much longer than most birders want to hear it; but, after all, it's not singing for the benefit of birders.

Our vireo builds a distinctive nest. It droops suspended between the forks of a branch, secured with spider web. The young must all leave the nest at once with the adult: any stragglers will be left behind. Unfortunately, these young sometimes consist of several cowbirds!

A migrant from South America, this vireo arrives in Atlanta in the spring, either nests here or goes on farther north, and in fall returns to its winter quarters.

Photos: Note the hook at the end of the thick bill and the striping through and above the eye. Bottom photo shows the plain breast. The red of the eye is not usually visible, as in these cases.

WHITE-BREASTED NUTHATCH
Sitta carolinensis
5"

What bird goes down a tree trunk head first? That acrobat is the white-breasted nuthatch. It searches for food in any direction: up, down, sideways. This spry little bird seems never to rest as it gleans spiders and insects from the trunks and large branches of trees.

Our nuthatch's breast and throat are white, as you'd expect from the name. On the hind underparts there's an area of buffy or rust, which might fool you into thinking you're looking at a RED-breasted nuthatch.

No, that bird (which is much rarer around here and not shown) has a deep rust on the actual breast, as well as a distinct black eye-stripe. Both birds, however, have black (female is dark gray) caps and shoulders, and gray wings.

The white-breasted's call announces its presence long before it may be visible: a loud, harsh, "quank-quank" or "yank-yank," given in twos and threes. What is generously called its song is a rapid series of notes on one pitch, amounting almost to a rattle.

This nuthatch abides year-round in our deciduous woodlots and leafy backyards. In winter it comes to feeders, where it stays about one second while it grabs a sunflower seed. It then opens the seed against the trunk of a tree.

Nesting is in natural cavities, boxes, or, rarely, under eaves. During nest preparation the male performs a bonding ceremony at the cavity hole, waving its bill and prancing about. The bird's five eggs are white with brown spray on the large end.

As common and easily identifiable as this bird is, it has been surprisingly hard to find on our Marietta Christmas Bird Counts. Be alert for it, however, almost anywhere in the Metro area where there are large hardwoods.

Photos: (Upper left) The male has a very dark cap while the female's (below) is grayer. Clearly visible (below) and faintly visible (above, right) is the rust on the hind underparts.

13

The little junco, or "snowbird" as some watchers call it, is always a welcome winter visitor. Sparrow-like, it seeks seeds on the ground, often under bird feeders. In the countryside, it gathers in flocks that flit through the tangled undergrowth or dart into the lower limbs of a tree.

The dark-eyed junco (to give its full name) is so widely variable in its North American range that it was formerly considered to be four different species. Older books give them as "white-winged," "slate-colored," "Oregon," and "gray-headed." These are now considered all one; only the "yellow-eyed' (formerly "Mexican") remains a separate species. Ornithologists change their minds about the classification of species from time to time as new information is gathered and published. What they're saying now is that all four of these forms can interbreed successfully with each other. By definition, where interbreeding stops, a new species begins.

In our range we have the former "slate-colored" form. It is white on the lower breast, dark gray (slate) above. A distinct demarcation occurs at mid-breast where light becomes dark. Mature males are darker than females, sometimes very dark, almost black, on the head. The seed-crushing bills are pinkish or white, with the thick conical shape characteristic of sparrows, to which juncos are close kin. Their outer tail feathers are white, a field mark you can easily see when the bird takes flight.

The junco's song -- which you'd be very lucky to hear in a north Georgia winter -- is a sweet trill. The nest (found in the north Georgia mountains) is a cup of bark and grass built right on the ground.

Photos: Male (above) shows dark gray or slate above and white below. The female (below) is a lighter gray than the male. White outer tail feathers are not easily visible until they fly.

The **house finch** originally lived only in the West. In 1940, it was brought to New York and released. In its new habitat, it spread like wildfire, eventually reaching Georgia. Then suddenly a natural enemy appeared: a bacterial eye disease. The house finches are currently in a bit of trouble from this. The upper breast and crown of the male house finch is tinged with crimson, variable to yellow. The female lacks the red altogether, being instead finely streaked with grayish brown on the underside and no pattern on the head.

You could confuse either sex of the house finch with those of the **purple finch** that are just frequent enough in Georgia to make you look twice or maybe three times. The color differences are not reliable, although the purple male finch is generally more raspberry. However, the sides of the male house finch have dark streaks, while the purple has none. Female purple finches (all brown, also lacking any red) have much heavier streaking than their counterparts, together with a clear face pattern: a broad dark band bordered with white. Purple finches are here only in the winter; they go back north in the spring and nest mostly in Canada

The house finch stays here year-round and vies with the feisty house sparrow for nesting holes in the crannies around shopping centers and malls, but they also like your hanging plants. They sing a bright, many-phrased/varied warble song.

You'll see them frequently at your feeder. Like other finches, they sit right there and eat their sunflower seeds, rather than fly away with them like a titmouse or chickadee. Watch as they crush the seed, letting the two husks fall away. A small flock will feed together rather peacefully on a tray feeder and then suddenly start squabbling with each other.

House finches are here to stay, provided they can develop immunity to their eye disease. On the other hand, purple finches are declining in numbers here in Georgia.

Photos: Top – male house finch (left) shows brown streaks below wings, whereas purple male finch (right) has none. Bottom -- the brown streaks of the drab female house finch (left) are narrow, and she has no face pattern; compare with the female purple finch showing thick breast streaks and bold white stripes behind and below the eyes.

The house sparrow is not a well-liked bird in the United States. It is an "exotic, import, immigrant, doesn't belong here." It takes other birds' nesting spaces such as the eastern bluebird and purple martin, for example. It is a scruffy, parking lot bird, a dingy city bird, a refuse-eater, surely too common for any self-respecting birder. Yet if you look with unbiased eyes at the male's striking breeding plumage, you'll have a visual treat. The crown is gray, nape chestnut, cheeks white, bib and bill black. The shoulder is chestnut with one white wingbar. That's a lot of exciting color all crowded into so small a place. The rest of the bird, of course, is just rather sparrow-looking; ditto for the female and juvenile.

Two common field guides don't deign to describe this bird's song. A third says "long series of monotonous musical chirps." Yes, that's about it, but they're distinctive musical chirps, and one can learn to recognize them. They sing throughout the year.

This bird is a weaver finch and is not closely related to our native sparrows. Eight pairs were introduced in Brooklyn in 1850 to help eat cankerworms. This group died out, but later reinforcements did well enough. The bird is now found throughout the country.

You almost never see these sparrows far from human habitation. They nest in any cavity they can find, often behind some fixture near a building. They bring in quantities of hay and grass, feathers, hair, string, whatever they can find. Two broods are usual. They've been known to lay eggs in other birds' nests. They're a scrappy and aggressive bird, often stealing from each other and getting into fights. They love dust baths.

It's a pleasure to see these wild birds skittering around on the asphalt of a parking lot as they search for fragments of waste food. Look at them closely and think good thoughts. They're one of our new "technobirds" and true survivors.

Photos: The breeding male (above) shows its black chin, chestnut wings, and white wingbar. Below is the much plainer female or juvenile.

The song sparrow loves the open country, but it can also be heard singing at in-town places, even near malls and parking lots. You will love the song once you come to recognize it. Think of the song as having three parts: some chips, some buzzes, some trills. With a bit of generosity you could grant the bird its specific name, melodia. Henry David Thoreau translated its song as "Maids! Maids! Maids! Hang up your teakettle-ettle-ettle." Thoreau was a very imaginative person.

The song sparrow can be recognized in a front view by the tendency of its breast streaks to radiate out from a central area in the middle of the lower neck, often forming a dark spot or splotch. This spot (when it actually exists) can be variable, and it, too, can engage the imagination. Sometimes you see it, other times you just think you see it. What to look for, then: heavy streaking on the breast, and a long, rounded tail. Also, song sparrows do not tend to form the large flocks so common, in winter, for field sparrows and chipping sparrows. They may appear, however, as individuals within such flocks.

You may like this sparrow because of its song, or because of the allure of its hypothetical breast spot. But this sparrow is very interesting for other reasons. It ranges widely in the United States. As it ranges, its characteristics vary, so that more than a dozen subspecies can be distinguished. These vary mainly in size, but also in bill shape, streaking, and over-all coloration. The various populations easily share their genes back and forth, so further speciation isn't likely right now. But given some new geographical barriers, together with a few tens of thousands of years, and this species might erupt into panoply of new kinds of sparrows.

Photos: The breast spot doesn't show -- often it doesn't. But still, notice the heavy streaking on the breast, from rusty brown to dark brown, which converges towards the throat. And you can see the very long tail, which gives you a good start in separating this species from other sparrows. Summer plumage (above) is brighter than winter plumage (below), which shows a lot of gray in the head pattern

TUFTED TITMOUSE
Baeolophus bicolor
5 ½"

A prominent gray crest distinguishes the titmouse from all others of this small size. Notice, too, the gray upper parts contrasting with the white breast. It has a rusty-colored patch on its side beneath the wing, and the stark black eye.

This is one of our most common birds around all neighborhoods, winter and summer. Normally the titmouse scours leaves for insects, actively flitting from place to place, even hanging upside down from twigs. But it is a reliable feeder bird, taking black oil sunflower seed consistently. Watch it take a seed, fly to a nearby twig, hold the seed with its feet, and peck it open. Back it will come for more, in less than a minute.

Titmice are close cousins to chickadees, and you'll frequently see two or three titmice in company with several chickadees. In breeding season, however, they are, like most other birds, territorial and anti-social. Tufted titmice nest in a tree cavity or sometimes in a small birdhouse.

Our bird has a sweet song much louder than you'd expect for such a small bird. It often sings "Peter Peter Peter," and is not above whistling "tweet tweet tweet." Squeaky squawks and sucking whistles are heard during food-begging and fighting.

If you are patient, you can gradually train a titmouse to take sunflower seeds from your hand. First let them learn to eat near you. It helps to have places nearby where the birds can perch while they're deciding whether to brave a possible trap. They may fear your eyes, so squint or close them at first. Be very still. Eventually they may come.

Photos: Titmouse on a suet feeder (above) showing its prominent crest. This very common little bird appears as a small gray bird with a long tail flitting through the trees. Its crest is a key identifying mark even at a distance, but occasionally it is not displayed (below); however, the gray above and light below along with the long tail are always apparent. The sexes are alike.

Here's the bird you've been waiting for. Societies and publications are devoted to it: the eastern bluebird. Once you see one in the glory of its vibrant sky blue, you'll be hooked.

The bluebird requires short grassy fields, in which it goes to the ground to catch its customary insect prey. For successful breeding it also needs very special kinds of cavities, not too large or too small, too high or too low. Human land use formerly caused a great decline in bluebird population. More recently, however, thanks to the sustained efforts of many dedicated individuals, bluebirds have made a comeback. Today they are once again a common sight in the open countryside.

The male's backside is an intense sky or cobalt blue. Just as often, though, you'll be glimpsing the rust-colored breast as it perches on a wire. Females and juveniles can show very little blue, so be ready to make your judgment by the rusty wash. Look for this bird on utility lines, fence wires, or the low limbs of trees in open areas.

Know also that bluebirds tend to remain all winter long in last year's family group of three or four. As a rule of thumb, any assemblage of a few small fat birds on a wire, spaced several feet apart from each other, will turn out to be bluebirds.

The bluebird song is slight and subtle, but sweet, and one you can learn to recognize. It's called 3 or 4 soft gurgling notes, which is fair for starters. You must hear it to know it.

Making nest boxes for bluebirds, or establishing bluebird trails around field edges, is a very exacting project. Obtain the proper information before you begin. Bluebirds are usually extremely particular.

Photos: Our views do not truly capture the glorious blue, but you see the general shape and form, and plenty of the rusty breast plus the short tail, fat belly. The male (above) is, as usual, much brighter and more colorful than the female (below).

19

DOWNY WOODPECKER	HAIRY WOODPECKER
Picoides pubescens	*Picoides villosus*
5 ¾"	7 ½"

The **downy** is our smallest woodpecker. In the suburbs, you're sure to see or hear it fairly often. It likes deep woods and dead trees as much as any woodpecker, but can make do with very little. You'll see it around your house, pecking food on the smallest of trees, or making a home in a dead branch stub that you wouldn't think fit for any bird. It is petite, busy, mottled black and white. The male has a tiny spot of red on the back of his head.

The song of the downy woodpecker is easy to recognize, and you'll begin to hear it often, once you catch on. It's a nasal whinny, starting high and then descending, not too loud. Nothing else like it out there. Unmistakable.

As with most woodpeckers, the downy finds its food by scouring the trunks and branches of trees. Preferring mid-height, it seldom comes near the ground, unlike its cousins the flicker, the hairy woodpecker, and the pileated woodpecker. It readily comes to suet feeders in winter, and in hard times even takes a fragment from the seed tray.

The **hairy woodpecker** – far less common than the downy – is like its cousin in appearance and habit, except that it is noticeably larger (medium size, not small). One can think of the downy as close to the size of a sparrow, while the hairy is more the size of a red-headed woodpecker or a cardinal.

Look at the bill: thick and long, dwarfing the downy's little stiletto. It's single-note chip call is more complex than the downy's. Also, it often feeds low at the bottoms of the trees or on fallen logs; another good reason to let some dead trees lie on the ground.

Photos: Top left, the male hairy; female shown below him. Top right, male downy; female below. Plumages are scarely distinguishable, but the size differs significantly. In particular, the bill for the hairy is as long as the head is wide, but the downy's bill length is not nearly as wide as the head; i.e., small bird, small beak.

There are many birds in the group called "flycatchers," most of which are very difficult to identify visually, and are not too frequently found. In fact, this group has the most bird species of any in the world. One that is likely to be seen regularly by bird watchers in Atlanta and the Piedmont area is the eastern phoebe. The other is the eastern wood-pewee (not shown).

We remember the phoebe, and have probably been aware of it all our lives, because we know it sings its old-fashioned name: a buzzy "fee-bee" or "flee-bee." The pewee sings its name too, but a slightly different name: a slurred, whistled "peeeo-weee."

The phoebe sits on twigs overlooking open spaces, often near a pond or wetland, and darts out to catch insects on the wing, then returns to its perch. It sits low in a bush or small tree, usually no more than six or eight feet above the ground. It enjoys the varied habitat of mixed-use farmland. It loves barbed wire fences, from which it can dart down into the stubble for some unlucky grasshopper.

The phoebe has good keys for identification. First, look for a solitary bird on a low perch doing some fly catching. Next, observe its black head, white throat, and breast very faintly washed with yellow. The back is dark gray. Lastly, but importantly, watch the tail. The phoebe will raise and lower its tail every few seconds. The pewee doesn't.

Phoebes like to nest underneath a natural or artificial structure: on a ledge beneath a rock overhang, under a dock.

Photos: The black head and white throat are very visible in both photos. You can also see the gray back, and a little of the vague yellow wash on the underparts, but not, of course, the wagging tail.

I saw a most distinguished, aristocratic bird today. What could it have been? Nothing but a cedar waxwing.

The sleek cedar waxwing, with its sharp crest and black mask, is indeed one of our most elegant birds. Brownish-amber overall, its tail is tipped with a band of yellow. You may see red waxy tips on some secondary wing feathers if you get a closer look at an adult.

Waxwings come to berry bushes in large, bubbly flocks, seeming to pounce on the bush from the sky. Then they strip it of berries, often leaving quite a mess beneath.

Flocking is what waxwings do best. Indeed, they are seldom seen singly except during breeding season, which comes late in the year after berries have ripened. Their flock is usually tight and well-controlled, wheeling this way and that with precision. In flight they could resemble starlings, but are smaller and browner.

Berries are the waxwings' staple, but they also eat insects. Their strangest food, however, is flower petals -- apple, for example, and tulip tree. In courting rituals, they pass these back and forth to each other. They nest in the mountains.

The waxwing's song is a high, thin, bell-like trilling, like the ringing of tiny chimes. You hear it not as an individual song, but as the music of an orchestra.

Photos: Both show the yellow-tipped tail and laid back crest. Upper view reveals the subtle breast colors, while lower photo shows the black mask and red-tipped wings. Absolutely beautiful bird.

WHITE-THROATED SPARROW
Zontrichia albicollis
5 ¾"

The white-throated sparrow is with us only during winter and early spring. Everyone who regularly feeds birds on the ground is apt to see it. This sparrow comes in small flocks of up to four, six, or eight. Its preferred times for scratching under your feeder are early in the morning and late in the evening, the same time at which most of the cardinals come. It pecks at small seeds awhile, then whisks away like the wind to nearby cover. During the day, it stays mostly out of sight, hiding in thick clumps of honeysuckle or privet along streams, or in tangles by brushy fencerows.

We recognize this bird best by its brown, sparrow-sized body and beak, plus the stark white throat. If you use binoculars, you'll also see a small yellow patch in front of its eye, a lore which becomes bigger and brighter as spring approaches. The back and wings are brown, but streaked with black. Breast is a faint gray with light streaking. This is an interesting dimorphic species because, like the screech-owl, it can appear in two forms: one with a bright black and white striped head pattern and one with a black and tan striped head pattern. It was thought originally that these represented male and female, respectively, just like many other bird species, but no, either form can be either sex.

Around the brushy parts of our yards, we recognize this bird by his call note. It's a single note: short, bright and bell-like, but a little raspy, as if the bell were cracked. When spring comes to the coast, and dogwoods bloom and native trees leaf out, the little white-throat becomes anxious to get back to its breeding grounds up north. At that time, you'll begin to hear the male's song, a plaintive whistled theme, sometimes described as "Old Sam Peabody, Peabody, Peabody." You'll hear that for a few days, a few weeks, then one day nothing: the bird is gone. We won't see or hear him again till next November.

Photos: (Upper) See the sharply delineated throat, white as the snow, and gray breast, and bright yellow lores. See also the black and white striping of the head. Note the white throat, gray breast, yellow lores, and crown. (Lower) You might think this a female with its more subdued colors, but for this species, both males and females can be either brightly colored or dull like this one.

23

Here's a bird you can rave about, one way or the other. Its black becomes an iridescent green, though to see the iridescence you must have the right light. Its strong beak is bright yellow in summer, dark in winter. In this season it is also speckled with white. Its wings appear very pointed in flight, and when it glides they appears swept-back like those of a jet fighter (see graphic, below).

Starlings are birds of ill repute because they're alien, and because they edge out some of our native birds. They were brought from Europe to New York in the late Nineteenth Century, and have spread rapidly across the country. This aggressive bird often steals the nest-cavities of native species. It is equally at home in city or farmland.

Starlings eat seeds, insects, fruit, garbage, i.e., they're omnivorous. They can be seen pecking their way across lawns or scavenging in parking lots. They may flock by themselves or with blackbirds. In mixed flocks, they can easily be distinguished by their stubby tails, pointed wings, and less intense black.

The starling's song is an interesting and not unpleasant assemblage of squeaks and whistles. The imitative myna bird is one of its kin.

One may feel chagrined that this bird is competing so successfully against certain American birds, such as the red-bellied woodpecker, from whom it steals. Considered by itself, however, the starling is as attractive a bird as many others.

Let's restrain our value judgments long enough to see the starling as a wondrous product of nature.

Photos: The winter male (above) shows wing feathers edged with brown that will wear away by summer, giving a blacker bird. Below, we see the yellow beak that is part of the spring breeding plumage. Again, speckles will yield to mostly solid black as the summer continues.

24

BROWN-HEADED COWBIRD
Molothrus ater
6 ½"

The brown-headed cowbird is one of the bird watcher's most hated birds, yet, for the same reason, one of the scientist's most interesting. It makes no nest of its own, but rather lays its eggs in the nest of another bird, often a warbler or other migrant. Its young take over the nest, usurping the energies of the step-parents, even ousting the legitimate offspring from their nest. It thus wreaks havoc on other species.

And yet this most unusual breeding strategy, similar to that of the European cuckoo, is worthy of study and perhaps even admiration. If only this fascinating bird was beautiful and rare, instead of plentiful and not particularly handsome, how differently might we view it.

In the past, the cowbird's range was restricted to the vast prairies of the West and Midwest. Like cattle egrets, the bird follows grazing animals to catch the insects they stir up. As agriculture and development opened up the woodlands of the eastern United States, the cowbird saw its chance and moved in. Now it is omnipresent, absent only from the deepest unbroken forests, which are few indeed. Thus rural development combines with the cowbird's spread to help cause the decline of our forest songbirds.

The mouse-colored female skulks around at dawn, waiting for her target bird to leave its nest. She darts in, lays a speckled egg, darts out. She may do this for several days, filling the host's nest with her foreign eggs. Sometimes the returning mother sees the ruse and ejects the intruder's egg; other times not. The cowbird's plan works only half the time, but it costs her nothing more than a few eggs.

The male is black, or greenish-black, with a brown head. Its bill is shorter and more sparrow-like than that of other blackbirds, with whom it often mixes. Its song is a short, squeaky whistle/gurgle; the female gives a soft, rattling chortle.

Photos: The cowbird's colors show well here: the female's (below) tan or gray, the male's (above) two-tone. See the male's iridescence, so common in blackbirds, making the black appear almost glossy blue.

25

ROSE-BREASTED GROSBEAK
Pheucticus lodovicianus
7 1/4"

For a short time in spring, many in our region get the thrill of a lifetime. Birds with striking red breasts descend on their feeders in little flocks to gorge on sunflower seed. They hand around a few short weeks before departing for their breeding grounds farther north.

If you crane your neck, you may see the bird high in the new-leafed trees. You're alerted to its presence by its song, which is much like a robin's only sweeter and more energetic. You may also hear its call, a short, squeaky "eek." Some compare it to the squeak of a tennis shoe on a slick floor.

You'll have no trouble identifying the male grosbeak. Its head, wings, and tail are coal black. The wings have white wingbars, and both the rump and stomach are white. The large, blunt seed-crushing bill is ivory colored. The red is shaped like a triangular bib. The female, however, is dull: brownish back and tail, white breast with brown streaks, large white eye-stripe above a dark cheek patch, and dull, washed-out golden yellow bill.

The grosbeak's nest is a weak saucer-shaped affair placed low in an elderberry or small oak. In the southern Appalachians, they nest in rhododendron. The male assists in brooding the eggs.

Our bird eats fruit and seeds, as well as cucumber and potato beetles and the larvae of many other pests.

The migratory rose-breasted grosbeak was added to this book by popular demand. Everyone was calling and asking: "What are theses gorgeous birds on my feeder?" Before 1997, the birds did no come to feeders so often. Why they have started coming now is not known.

Photos: Male (above) shows the eye-catching red breast, which is distinctive even from a distance. Female (below) shows large bill and broad white eye-stripe. Both sexes have chunky bodies compared with most species.

RED-WINGED BLACKBIRD
Agelaius phoeniceus
7 ¼"

The red-winged blackbird nests in wetlands and beside streams and ponds. In winter it joins other blackbirds to form vast flocks that roam the Southeast, foraging in fields and yards. Farmers in the area consider it a pest. Its flocks can fill the sky like wisps of smoke. Watch a large flock of mixed black birds feeding in your yard for "rolling": birds at the rear fly to the front where there is fresh food; in this manner the flock inches forward.

The black males of the species flaunt a red-orange patch on the wing-bend called an "epaulet," a military term. It is the bird's distinguishing mark. In breeding season it gets redder than ever, showing like a wondrous glow, especially when the male spreads its wings in mating display. Immature males in winter flocks show only a pale yellowish bar, not the red. Females are entirely different. They're all brown, with a breast heavily-streaked. You could mistake them for sparrows of some kind, but not if you notice the large blackbird bill!

How do you tell a redwing in a big flock of black-colored birds if you can't make out the red wing patch? Here are comparisons. Common grackle: the redwing is smaller, and has a smaller bill. In flight, it clearly lacks the grackle's large, wedge-shaped tail. Starling: the redwing does not have that swept-wing, jet-plane look. Cowbird: the redwing is bigger, with a black head instead of a brown one.

The aggressive and protective male, in breeding season, produces a very nice song: "oke-a-lee." In overhead flight, redwings give out a quiet "chuck" call.

The smallish nest is lashed to wetlands shrubs and tall grasses. The young can climb and swim even before they can fly. There may be several broods in a summer.

Photos: The red-orange epaulet of the male (above) has a yellow border that may or may not be prominent. The female (below) looks like an entirely different species, with her brown, heavily-streaked breast. In winter, you may see the females in a flock all by themselves and scratch your head before you think, "redwing!" When the females are with the males, however, you can make the red-wing connection easily.

27

Here's a bird whose call ("to-weee") sounds very much like "tweet" and also like its own name. The male's spring song is "drink-your-tea-eee," but often it says only part of that, and sometimes the "tea" is a whistle.

Our towhee is a ground bird, and kin to the sparrows. It scratches around among the leaves looking for seeds and insects. The male has a striking black back, white belly, and rufous sides. The female is the same, except the upper part is brown instead of black. Their eyes are red-orange.

Watch how the towhee continually flicks its tale, spreading it open so the two hidden white feathers show. This white-spot-flicking is just as much a part of the physical appearance of the bird as any other feature, so be alert for it.

Towhees will come to bird-mix spread on bare ground, and sometimes fly up to a feeder. Like brown thrashers, the only time they seek height is when they're singing in the spring.

A pair of towhees feeding in the same vicinity will keep in contact with each other by making frequent chips and calls. The towhee's nest, which is near the ground, is well concealed and difficult to find.

Even though towhees are tolerant of suburban development, their numbers are on the decline. Because of their ground- loving habits, perhaps these birds are more vulnerable than most to neighborhood cats.

Photos: Top left shows the black-headed male towhee in his familiar ground habitat; above right, singing on his spring territory. Below is the browner colored female.

The red-headed woodpecker is striking for its black and white wing pattern and dark red head. No other woodpecker has the solid red head. Yet people often mistakenly give its name to the red-bellied woodpecker, whose head is the color of an orange-red Crayola and only on the top, not the whole head. The juvenile red-head, which you might happen to see in mid-summer, is different: its head is gray-brown, and its wings are not quite as black.

Like most other woodpeckers, the red-headed searches trees for insects hiding in or under the bark. Or it may dig for a woodborer grub. Working hard and taking turns, the male and female can hollow out their nest hole in a matter of days. It prefers to build high in a dead pine, often in a swampy area. In the city, it likes large hardwoods growing not too close together, such as in a park or along a street.

It would probably use our dead pines if we left a few standing. In winter this woodpecker will take sunflower seeds from a tray feeder, or go to suet on the side of a tree. On the tray, it is feisty and selfish, often attacking other birds with its spear-like beak.

The red-headed woodpecker sings loudest in spring, when rivalries give rise to raucous singing contests. But it's not much of a song: a rasping-whirring kind of noise, or a barked nasal squawk. It will drum loudly on a tree to stake out its territory.

This species is declining throughout its range, possibly because starlings, a non-native species, drive it from its nesting cavities in many cases.

Photos: The stark contrast between the black and white of the wings is equally evident in flight as well as when it is on a tree trunk. Male and female are alike, but the immature shown in the inset has a dark brown head, which slowly molts to red during the first winter. Note: the holes seen in the tree are from a yellow-bellied woodpecker, not the red-headed.

"Redbirds" we call them in the South because of their nearly unmistakable brilliant red plumage and red-orange beaks. So common are they that we take them entirely for granted, yet people have traveled thousands of miles to see this striking red beauty. They are absent in the West.

The sexes are different. The male is almost completely red except for a grayish wash over the wings. The female is duller with a more brownish or grayish coloration. A juvenile of either sex looks like the female except that the juvenile's beak is brown, not red-orange.

The heavy mandibles of the cardinal show immediately that it is adapted to crushing seeds, not spearing insects. That beak can draw blood from a human's finger. Watch as the bird goes through a pile of sunflower seeds. Seed husks drop out of the sides of its beak as it grinds back and forth.

Cardinals will turn up anywhere and are certainly adapted to our suburbs. However, they seem to like swampy woods best. In winter, when they aren't being territorial, flocks of thirty or more have been counted at some feeding stations. The range of the cardinal has expanded northward as more food is provided during winter by bird lovers.

Cardinals sing mostly in spring, when you'll hear their pleasant "kyeeer, kyeeer" or "purty, purty, purty." At other times, they utter a single metallic chip note, which you can easily learn to recognize with a little practice.

The novel The Cook describes redbird hunts with gourmet feasts following. Fortunately, it is now against the law to kill or harass any songbird or even to possess a feather of one. Feathered hats were one of the original causes of decimated bird populations.

Photos: High crest, orange bill, and black face distinguish this male as he guards his territory (above). The female (below) is rather gray with a few faint washes of red and reddish on wings and tail.

YELLOW-BELLIED SAPSUCKER
Sphyrapicus varius
7 ¾"

While this name may be used when downgrading someone you dislike, it is quite appropriate for this woodpecker with its yellowish underparts. It also has the typical plump body and stout-pointed beak of other woodpeckers along with a red patch on a part of its head — in this case, the forehead. The male also has a red throat patch and the female differs by having a white throat patch. The most distinctive identification feature is a broad white wing patch running from the shoulder almost half way down the wing, and this can be picked out from a distance.

The yellow-bellied sapsucker migrates the most of any woodpecker in the eastern U.S. It spends its winters in the southeast, and then heads back to Canada to breed during the spring and summer. There is essentially no overlap in its summer and winter ranges.

During its winter in the southeast, it may move around considerably from area to area, or it may pick a tree it particularly likes and peck row upon row of regularly spaced, fairly deep holes in the trunk. It then uses its brush-like tongue to lick out the sap flowing into the holes, thus deriving its name. Ants and other insects also come to the sap, so the sapsucker includes these in its diet, as well. Only the sapsucker woodpecker consumes over 50% of its diet from a plant source rather than an animal (insect) source. Unfortunately, damage and even death to the tree can result when the sapsucker continues to produce hundreds of holes in it.

This woodpecker is generally quiet in the winter, but can produce a cat-like note of mewing or whining (sounding like a downward slurred "cheeerrrrr") that is also distinct and identifies it without seeing it. It tends to be shy and hides behind the tree trunk when humans are around.

Photos: Above is a view of the male defined by his red throat that the female (below) lacks. The yellowish underparts are clear. Note that both male and female have red caps on the head. Both views show the white wing patch that helps to identify this species of woodpecker. Note also the regular pattern of holes that they have pecked into the bottom tree trunk to obtain sap.

The eastern screech owl is a small chunky bird, no more than eight inches high, but with a wingspan of nearly two feet. It is usually a rusty reddish brown with white markings on the wings and chest. It can be gray, however, and rarely a drab brown. Different color phases or "morphs" like this occur in several species of birds. The causes are as yet unclear.

In our area screech owls show up wherever there are trees with cavities. Common though they are, they conceal themselves well. You're more likely to hear one than see it. Most of their singing is done in spring and summer. One song is a descending trill or whinny, another is a low monotonous rattle, very soft. When protecting their young from intruders they make strange barks and popping sounds.

Screech owls eat birds, small rodents, and large insects. They attack silently on wings muffled by fuzzy featheredges, making no more noise than a butterfly.

Many people render screech owls more observable by placing nest boxes in their yards. A good box might be eight inches square, twelve high, with a three- inch hole at the upper end. Owls don't want a perch and don't need nest material. Place the box twelve feet high, or as high as your ladder will reach.

Owls occupy the boxes as early as December. In late afternoon, or even in midday, the owls may bask in the box opening where you can get a good look at them. Young, two or three, will fledge in May or June. The chicks have gray, downy feathers. Sometimes during the day songbirds will discover a screech owl roosting in a thicket or under a canopy of vines. They then "mob" the owl, fussing loudly and hopping around excitedly. The owl usually endures this nuisance stolidly.

Photos: Rusty brown (above, and below, left) is typical of the eastern screech owl. The gray phase (below, right) is less common in the South. The gray owl has its "ears" flattened; the other two have them raised. Note yellow irises.

KILLDEER
Charadrius vociferous
8"

The killdeer, a kind of plover, is one of the few shorebirds that we regularly see or hear in Atlanta. Other shorebirds are found inland on migration, and may turn up at lucky spots, but killdeer are with us all the time.

The killdeer is easy to identify by its two black bands on a white breast. The back and head are dull brown, but the rump shows a bright rusty color in flight. Its song resembles its English name: "kill-dee." You can recognize it far away by its piercing piping or whistled notes, "te-te-de-dit, de-dit."

Open fields and pastures are its favorite feeding grounds, but you may also see it by river and lake banks, and, not so surprisingly, at the beach. It occurs singly, although on Christmas Bird Counts it can be found in loose grazing flocks of ten or fifteen, where it searches the grass for worms, crickets, and grasshoppers.

This bird nests in gravelly places, easily adapting to driveways and flat rooftops. It makes a "scrape" where its eggs lie bare to the sky" though they are well camouflaged. The fuzzy young chick (with just one neck stripe) is "precocial" -- ready for action as soon as it hatches. What the killdeer is perhaps most famous for is its "broken wing" feinting behavior. It lures four-legged predators away from its nest by dragging its wings, as if injured, and piping plaintively. Just when the cat or fox is sure of an easy meal, the mother bird flies away. Other birds perform this trick too, though none is as famous for it as the killdeer.

The killdeer is often active at evening, making it a "crepuscular" bird. Listen for it after supper on your next camping trip.

Photos: The short stubby beak and blunt forehead are typical of plovers. Brown back and wings, white underparts and relatively long legs. Look especially at the black and white breast bands: two black, two white.

The beauty of the eastern meadowlark is enough to make your heart melt. Fortunately for us they are plentiful, but only in the open country. It's worth taking a spring or summer tour of our outlying farmlands just to catch sight and sound of them.

Before you ever see them, their song will win you over. Let's go with this description: a clear, whistled "see you- see-yeeer," with the last part down-slurred. So sweet, so clarifying, so uplifting. Their call, a guttural noise you wouldn't associate with them at all: "dzrrt," with some chatter. Listen for that too in the fields, and realize it's coming from the same bird.

Meadowlarks are usually seen in small flocks of five, ten, or fifteen. When they take flight, recognize them by the white feathers on either side of the tail. When they glide in for a landing in a field, they remind you of certain fighter jets with down-slanted wings. Perched on a fence post or wire, facing you, there's no mistaking them: bright yellow breast with a black vee. When facing the other way, however, they show you only brown. Notice the large pointed beak, which puts them in the blackbird family, kin to redwings and grackles.

Eastern and western meadowlarks are an example of a species that has recently split into two from some more ancient parent species. Outwardly they are difficult to distinguish; their voice, however, tells them apart. The birds themselves know their differences, and do not interbreed, even when their ranges overlap in Texas and the Southwest.

Meadowlark nests are built right on the ground, sometimes with growing grass interlaced over the roof. Average territory for a nesting pair is seven acres. Farm equipment destroys many nests, but fallow fields and edges allow the species to persist despite human activities. Both adults and young eat insects of all kinds, and, in autumn and winter, waste seeds and grain.

Photos: Perching, the meadowlark shows his yellow breast with its black vee blotch; white side tail feathers are just barely visible. Lower photo shows the brown back, long bill, and how well the bird fits its background when the breast is more hidden.

When robin redbreast sings his very best, that's springtime. Fortunately robins are with us all year long, hopping on the ground, sometimes singing, nesting at the appointed time. What could be a better song than their springtime "cheerily cheer-up cheerio?" What could be a better sight than robins hustling in the snow?

Most people are familiar with robins: tawny red breast, dark back with black head. The females are a little duller than the males. Juveniles sport speckled breasts in summer and have a gawky quality that provides a treat in summer.

You can chance upon robins almost anywhere: in fields and yards, in orchards and woods. Usually they stay low down, because they feed on the ground, eating worms and bugs. Don't expect them to be interested in the seed at your feeder.

A robin's nest is made of twigs and straw bonded with mud or clay, out on a branch ten or twenty feet high. There could be bits of plastic mixed in. The eggs are a beautiful sky-azure. Robins often have two or more broods every spring or summer.

When you see a robin cock its head at the ground, run a little way, stop, cock again, what's it doing? Listening? A scientist decided to find out, so she lay down on the ground herself to see what she could hear. Instead, she discovered that she could see a lot of things -- insects. So then that was what the robin was probably doing: looking.

Robins are found in flocks both large and small. A few years back a flock observed during a Christmas Count was tallied at one million birds! But more often you see them grouped as five, ten, or twenty birds. Do you know how to identify them when they're flying overhead? By their spacing: they seem to like staying ten or fifteen feet apart.

Photos: Upper picture shows a spring male searching for insects, while the lower photo is of a female with a typical meal: a worm. Note the male's very dark head. Both sexes have a broken white eye-ring, and yellow bill.

RED-BELLIED WOODPECKER
Melanerpes carolinus
8 ½"

The red-bellied is such a common woodpecker in our area that you've surely seen or heard one in your back yard. The head of the male is bright orange-red. At your first meeting with this bird you might possibly think you were seeing the red-HEADED woodpecker; that bird, however, has a very dark, entirely red head, with striking black and white wings.

From a distance our fellow has a grayish appearance (our eye blends its fine black and white mottling). Some people call it a "ladder-back" because of that striped mottling. At a second look you'll notice that the whole head isn't orange-red, just the back and top of it. The cheeks are the same light buffy color as the belly. The female has even less red, just the back part of the head.

This woodpecker's call is a rattle or chortle, intoned in various ways. Practice is needed to tell its sounds from those of the red-headed. Sometimes you must listen twice to be sure it's not a kingfisher or a great crested flycatcher.

Its habits are those of most woodpeckers. It digs its nest hole in a dead tree snag. There it lays eggs that are round and white, like those of most cavity-dwellers. It spends its time on the trunks of trees searching for insects. In spring it stakes out a territory by drumming. It drums on whatever makes a good loud noise, including gutters and sides of houses.

The red-bellied woodpecker willingly takes sunflower seeds from a feeder, where it sometimes fights for sole possession. It opens these seeds by placing them in a crack of tree bark and pecking. It also goes after suet.

The flight of most woodpeckers is described as "undulating," because they flap in spurts. Between spurts you can see the body arcing like a dart, wings folded. Knowing how woodpeckers fly, you can spot one a mile away.

Photos: Note that the red-bellied has red only on the crown and nape, not on the cheeks and throat. Note, too, the black and white striping on the back, which from a distance blends into gray. Upper left photo is the female, on the right the male. The male's red covers the whole top of the head (below left), whereas the female's stops at the eye, leaving her bald-looking (below right).

NORTHERN MOCKINGBIRD
Mimus polyglottos
9"

This is the state bird of Florida, Mississippi, and Texas and is very common throughout the South. It is "northern" only to South America! Of all the suburban avian singers, probably none can rival the mockingbird. Its own specific song is long and complicated. Meanwhile, it mimics other birds, as well as snatches of noise from the surrounding environment. There can be times when you truly do not know whether you're hearing another bird, or the imitation of it by the mocker. And does it sing! Endlessly at times, even for hours, even at night, particularly in spring. The call is a harsh "tchack."

The mockingbird will repeat phrases of its song many times, often in groups of threes. Its cousin, the brown thrasher, sings various notes in doublets. The other cousin, the darker gray catbird, sings a garbled song of single notes with little repetition. These three species together are our "mimids," so-called from their mimicking abilities.

While some birds get pushed aside by the advance of civilization, the mockingbird thrives on it. The more TV aerials the better. The more little starter trees on a lawn of manicured grass, better still. House cats? A mere distraction.

The mockingbird is an over-all gray, with accents of black and white. It has a habit of flexing and extending its wings, showing large white patches. You see these too when it flies, along with white edges on the tail. A sleek gray bird with white wing flashes is bound to be a mocker.

Mockers build their nest within ten feet of the ground, and attack anything coming near it. Best tactic for this bird is to learn to appreciate this very special species, for it seems destined to survive every obstacle we throw at it.

Photos: Note the over-all gray color with lighter chest. The body is sleek with a long tail that is typically cocked in the air. The flashing white wing patches only show when the bird is flying or using the wings for hunting insects as shown in the inset.

BROWN THRASHER
Toxostroma rufum
10"

Our Georgia state bird belongs to the same family as that great imitator, the mockingbird. The brown thrasher, however, seldom copies other birds' songs. Its own song, performed in spring from a perch twenty or thirty feet high, is a series of notes usually sung in pairs. From low in the bushes, especially at evening and early morning, it will also utter a sharp "chuck" or shushing hiss.

At a distance, a thrasher darting across a shadowy country road could be confused with a female cardinal. But the thrasher is rustier, larger, and has a longer tail. The tail is often pointed smartly upwards, as in the photos below. Notice also the boldly streaked breast, long curved beak, white wingbars, and pale yellow eye. Another brown bird with a speckled breast is the wood thrush, which migrates through our area in spring and fall, often staying the summer; that bird, however, has a brown (not yellow) eye, white eye-ring, and a much shorter tail.

Brown thrashers are ground birds, except in spring when the males sing from perches. The rest of the time they scratch in the leaves, shuffling and overturning them with gusto. They can run quite fast along the ground. Insects and fruit comprise most of their diet. They are not common at bird feeders, but may occasionally take some seed from the ground.

The egg of the thrasher is a wonderfully shaped and mottled thing, but it takes luck and skill to find the thrasher's clutch hidden low in the bushes. Of course, if it nests in the hedge by your mailbox, it's yours for the viewing.

One of John James Audubon's most dramatic paintings shows four brown thrashers ganging up together to protect a nest of eggs from a marauding black rat snake. Nowadays thrashers are much more likely to be destroyed by feral cats running loose in the neighborhood than by snakes.

Photos: The sexes are alike. In both photos, notice rusty brown coloration of wings and back, the long, uptilted tail, breast streaking, yellow eye, and a beak meant for business.

Jays of various kinds are found throughout the country, but the only one in our area is the blue jay. It belongs to the Corvid family, which includes crows and magpies. All of these are noisy, raucous, mischievous birds that are smart and given to being scavengers and opportunists. A blue jay will eat anything from birdseed at a feeder to eggs or babies in a nest.

The blue jay averages ten inches in length. Its head crest is quite distinctive most of the time. If you look closely, you'll see that it's blues are remarkable: mauve, blue-gray, blue, and turquoise. The black and white markings are striking. The underside is gray, turning to white under the base of the tail ("undertail coverts").

Our jay likes to build its nest at a fork near the trunk of a tree. In early spring it may construct one or two practice nests before starting on the real one. It likes to build with wet leaves from a bog, but will use other materials too. It behaves very quietly around its nest, hopping slowly towards it from branch to branch, in order to fool predators. It needn't fool you though: just watch for jays carrying nest material.

Jays are famous for squawking loudly at cats and snakes, but their favorite targets are crows, hawks, and especially owls. A flock of eight or ten jays will make a great horned owl really nervous, flying past it and sometimes actually striking the big bird's head and feathers. When you hear mobbing jays giving their harshest, most frenzied calls, go see if there isn't an owl or hawk nearby.

You may not be aware that the blue jay has a short, sweet, flute-like song. It also gives a throaty rattle when it isn't happy.

Photos: The color of a blue jay can vary from bright blue to a purple-gray, depending on light conditions. Its blues are the result of refraction, not pigmentation.

39

MOURNING DOVE
Zenaida macroura
10 ½"

One bird watcher in the Southeast who each day listed the birds he saw claimed to have seen a mourning dove every single day of the year. Are they really that common? Not necessarily. But you have surely seen one already.

In spring and summer, doves make a mournful cooing sound from low dense shrub, or from their perches high in the pines, where they build their flat, flimsy nests. Unlike the many species that feed their young on insects, doves nourish their chicks by regurgitation mouth to mouth, poking their heads right down the chick's gullet. Adults eat small seeds, even the minute seeds of violets. You see by their beaks that they lack the crushing power of finches, cardinals, and sparrows.

The mourning dove has a tan body with brown and gray wings and gray tail. Here and there is a spot of black. You may see some iridescence, especially around the neck and head that seems small in comparison with the body. Beak is slim and slightly down-turned. Strange and special: hear the wings squeak when they fly! The flight is swift and direct, with wings beating quickly and long pointed tail trailing behind.

On the ground the bird walks methodically, pecking at seeds in the open, moving its head back and forth rather like a chicken. It appears either to be either unable or unwilling to scratch the ground or turn over leaves.

Don't think of the dove as necessarily a bird of peace, for on the feeder it will raise its wings in threat and chase off other birds, including those of its own species.

Mourning doves are classed as a game bird, suitable for hunting as sport. This puts them in a class with turkey, quail, pheasant, and duck. No wonder the doves we see at our city feeders are very wary: in south Georgia they are fair game for hunters with shotguns. In Atlanta, they are preyed upon by hawks, owls, and feral cats.

Photos: The wing is light, brownish-gray with black blobs. Tail is long, very pointed in flight. Neck seems long and head small. Bill is slim and down-curved. Male and female look alike.

What's that largish brown bird with the white rump that flies up from the lawn? It's the northern flicker, a member of the wood-pecker family. Until recently we called it the "yellow-shafted" flicker, for it shows a flash of bright yellow on the underside of its wings. A similar bird in the West was called the "red-shafted". Zoologists decided these were the same species, so they re-named both birds (along with the gilded) as northern flicker. This sort of thing happens from time to time as scientists gradually learn more about species.

Our flicker has a black bib and a red swatch on the back of its head. The belly is strongly spotted with black. The male has a black moustache, the female, none. If you see several together on a tree trunk during mating season, check for moustaches to determine the birds' sex. Then you'll know what sort of interaction you're witnessing -- love or war.

In breeding season you can hear flickers singing "wicker-wicker-wicker." There are many variations on this. It advertises its territory with a short, sharp, screaming cackle. Flickers also have a one-note call, a harsh "screep," used year-round.

Ants are one of this bird's favorite foods. Their long tongues are good for lapping up both workers and grubs. But they eat other insects, too. Berries, including poison ivy, make up a large portion of their diet.

Flickers are common in our suburbs. Elsewhere they prefer the edges of swamps, or open areas with just a few trees. Like other woodpeckers, they ordinarily nest in cavities, usually drilled out by themselves.

In earlier times flickers were hunted, for they are good to eat. Nowadays their greatest enemies are owls, hawks, cats, and cars.

Photos: Male sports a black moustache (upper), female (below) does without. Both have black breast-band, speckled breast, and red dash on the back of the head. Flickers can be seen frequently on the ground looking for insects as shown above.

Not counting crows, the largest blackbird we see around Atlanta is the common grackle. Sometimes called "purple grackle", our grackle may show a bronze or purplish or bluish or greenish sheen in various lights. Admire the color, but don't bother too much about it as a guide to identification. Instead, look for the long tail widening toward the end.

Grackles often come in huge flocks that descend on your lawn and cover the ground. You can hear their noisy squeaking and creaking, and watch them turn over leaves in search of nuts and seeds. They especially prefer small acorns such as those of the water oak. In fact, they have a special ridge on their upper mandible that helps them crack the nuts open.

On the ground, grackles really strut, as if they thought they owned the place. Yet they startle easily. The whole flock may fly up all at once just because you raised your window shade or opened the back door.

The long tail of the grackle has some people comparing it to a "keel". Their beaks are large and their eyes pale yellow. Their official sound, according to some, is "koguba-leek".

Grackles flock with other blackbirds with which the grackles might be confused. Notice, then, that red-winged blackbirds are considerably smaller, and will have a crescent of red or orange or white on their shoulder. Starlings will be short and chunky, with hardly any tail at all, and you may see the pretty speckling on them. Cowbirds will be much smaller than grackles, black with a brown head (males) or mousy gray (females).

The common grackle is smaller than the boat-tailed grackle, which is found on Georgia's coast, and they are much quieter and more well-behaved.

In winter, grackles cross the sky in huge flocks, often in long wavy lines. Other blackbirds may be mixed with them including red-wings, starlings, and cowbirds. Forget the saying "Birds of a feather flock together"! Look to see what's there.

Photos: Bird may appear bluish-black (above) or purplish-black (below), according to the light. In either case, note wide tail and pale eye.

Field guides list four species of pigeon (*Columba*) for the United States: band-tailed pigeon, red-billed pigeon, white-crowned pigeon, and rock dove. The first three are highly restricted in range, but we see the rock dove in nearly every town. We know it simply as a "pigeon."

Pigeons are excellent fliers, being quite beautiful as they wheel and turn in flocks. In some cities people raise them in cages on roof tops and have contests and "wars" with each other's flocks.

Guess what famous person raised pigeons? Charles Darwin! "Believing that it is always best to study some special group, I have, after deliberation, taken up domestic pigeons." It turns out that there are many different breeds of pigeon, some very strange: carrier, short-faced tumbler, runt, barb, pouter, turbit, Jacobin, trumpeter, laugher, and fantail, to name the most important.

Pigeons inhabit cities because the stone and concrete buildings are like the rocks on which the ancestral wild species lived. All the pigeons in the United States are descended directly from imported domesticated pigeons.

Our rock doves come in many colors: white, reddish-brown, and black, with gray-blue being the most common; and there are mixtures. But the birds have a tendency to revert to the ancestral form. Let Darwin describe that form: "I crossed some uniformly white fantails with some uniformly black barbs, and they produced mottled brown and black birds; these I again crossed together, and the one grandchild of the pure white fantail and pure black barb was of as beautiful a blue color, with the white rump, double black wing-bar, and barred and white-edged tail-feathers, as any wild rock-pigeon!"

Instead of downgrading or ignoring our common pigeons, let's admire their iridescent colors and enjoy their swift flight and aerial acrobatics.

Photos: The bird above shows a bird with black, iridescent and gray parts plus the bright orange feet – just one example of a mixture of colors that can be anything from pure black to pure white on different birds. Below is the most typical coloration: dark, iridescent neck, red eye, light gray back and wings, two dark wingbars.

Our belted kingfisher ranges widely over the entire United States. Lakes, rivers, and streams -- even small ones -- are its home. It feeds by diving headfirst into the water, taking fish sometimes as long as itself, which it swallows whole. It usually fishes from a perch near the bank. Occasionally it will hover like an osprey. They sometimes perch on power lines near water. Upon taking a fish, it is not unusual to see them bash it against their perching limb quite a few times before swallowing it.

The belted kingfisher has a conspicuous white breast with blue-gray back, wings, and crest. There is also a breast-band of the same color. The female has a second, lower, breast-band, of rust-red. The beak and head are large in relation to the body, and the crest on the head is noticeable even at a distance.

The bird's call is a thin, dry rattle which it usually gives as it flies over the water in its characteristic erratic manner.

Kingfishers are solitary except when paired for nesting. Their nest is a deep hole dug into the side of a clay bank. The sexes take turns digging, sometimes as far into the bank as fifteen feet. When one mate comes to relieve the other on the nest, it calls from a nearby perch, then waits for the mate to leave before entering.

Kingfishers love to fly up and down streams. If the stream is covered with a tree canopy, they fly it as if through a tunnel, rattling as they go.

Photos: The male is shown above eating a freshly caught fish; the single breast band is a little hard to see. The female with its second rusty breast-band is shown below. Different lighting conditions produce different hues of blue for the back, but the large, shaggy crests are unmistakable.

The wood duck is less common in our area than the mallard, but far prettier once you find it. The male's head is distinguished by a crest that falls down over the back of the neck like a ponytail. The top of his head is green, eye and base of bill red, cheek black with white stripes, breast brown with fine light speckles, side white, back and tail black. In flight, that finery will be hard to see. Instead, look at the shape of the head: the bill will be down-turned. The less-colorful female is brown, with a wide, distinct, white eye-ring. Listen for her alarm call, given in flight: a piercing "whoo-eek."

Wood ducks almost became extinct in the early Twentieth Century, as many people wanted their feathers for finery or desired stuffed specimens. Now they've made a good comeback, due in large part to a program of putting nest boxes for them in the middle of ponds and swamps.

You've seen those: on poles, usually protected from raccoons by a metal cone. Otherwise, the birds nest in tree hollows or large woodpecker holes, in which they lay fifteen or twenty white eggs.

Wood ducks may walk quietly through the forest floor around their swamp, eating acorns. In the water, they dabble on the surface, eating insects and duckweed. They're found in the most wild and beautiful places: thick swamps with moss draping off the branches.

Since they have the ability to take off straight up without spatting across the water, they can feel safe even in tight places. You may find them on some of the slow-moving creeks and beaver ponds in the city. Usually they see you before you see them, so be prepared for their surprising burst into the air, and their eerie cry as they vanish through the treetops.

Photos: Note particularly the shape of the male's head, with its high forehead, its crest looking almost like a backwards bill, and much white striping on black along with all the other beautiful coloring. Below, with her lack of bright colors, the female's large, distinct white eye-ring is a good field mark for her

45

Fish constitute the diet of many kinds of birds. One source of small fish is freshwater streams, lakes, and swamps. Some birds (kingfishers, ospreys, bald eagles) take fish right out of the middle of such waters. Other birds hunt along the shoreline, going in only as deep as their long legs will take them (egrets, herons). One short-legged fish bird stakes out the shallowest places of all, and sometimes even hunts from a dry limb just above the water's surface: the green heron.

The deceptive thing about our bird is its neck. Perched, or coiled for a strike at its prey, it seems to have no neck at all. That is an illusion, for as it strikes, or as it rises in flight, it stretches its neck to truly heron-like lengths.

The chest and shoulders, which constitute half the surface area of this heron, are a deep, rusty brown. The wings are a dark bronze that, with generosity and imagination, is termed green. In breeding season the legs are a bright golden orange, otherwise, pale greenish or ochre.

The loud call of this heron is distinctive and easy to recognize: a harsh, sharp "skeow" or "kyowk."

Green herons nest alone or in a small colony, building their nests ten or twenty feet above the ground. They have mating rituals and displays as other birds do: raising of crests and plumes, crouching, bill snapping. We don't ordinarily hope to see that. We'd be quite satisfied just to see one fishing.

Photos: The specimen in the lower photo sports its orange breeding legs, chestnut breast, and the back feathers that we have all agreed to call green, but looks bluish in the upper photos. You see the large beak, proficient for spearing, and, in the upper left photo, the long neck that drives it. Upper right photo shows more typical posture the bird uses while hunting fish. Both postures are normal, as is the habitat: shoreline or low branches. The birds above have pale yellow legs typical of females and non-breeding males.

PILEATED WOODPECKER
Dryocopus pileatus
15"

The pileated woodpecker is a truly magnificent replacement for its recently-extinct cousin, the ivory-bill. Early woodsmen, with good reason, dubbed it the "gawd-almighty." Big as a crow, with almost as much black, it glides into your woodlot like a dream or vision. It may peck at a hole it wants for a nest. It may course the trunk of a tree up and down, looking for ants or other insects. More likely, it will fly right down to the ground to tear apart a rotten log. It flakes off huge chunks with its large chisel beak. Grubs and beetles it will take, centipedes and millipedes, spiders, and all; but what it really craves are large, black carpenter ants. "Log cock" is one of its local names.

The pileated woodpecker was the bird "Woody Woodpecker" was modeled after. It gets its name, pronounced with a short "i", from its conspicuous red crest (pileus). The bird is noisy, with a loud, crazy cackle that rings through the woods: ten to fifteen "kuks." The feeding peck (as distinct from territorial drumming) is loud and slow with no rhythm. Its flight pattern as it crosses the open spaces of roads and fields is a distinctive one which you can learn with a little practice. Practice is needed, too, to separate its song from that of the flicker (whose cackle is shriller and faster).

The pileated hollows out a deep nest in a sufficiently large dead tree or snag. The vertically-oval hole is three to four inches in diameter, making it suitable for future use by a screech owl. Its eggs -- like those of most cavity-nesters -- are white and round. But you won't find the shells at the base of the tree, as that would alert predators to the presence of the nest.

The pileated woodpecker is fairly common in our towns, as well as relatively unwary. Feeding with little regard for human intruders, it often allows a close approach. But whether you view it with naked eye or with binoculars, the look is always spectacular.

Photos: Note the solid black wings, tail, and body. See the red moustache behind and below the bill of the male (upper photo). The female (below) has a black moustache. Both sexes have a bright red crest.

COOPER'S HAWK
Accipiter cooperii
15 ½"

The Cooper's hawk is probably less well known to most people than the red-tail hawk. It is smaller, with shorter wings but a longer tail. When mature, the breast is reddish with horizontal barring, and the back slate-gray. Immatures have a light breast with vertical streaking, and a brown back. You're lucky to see a Cooper's hawk in a day's birding in Georgia, luckier still to hear its shriek or its cack-cack-cack-cack.

Hawks are a confusing group at first, but with persistence you can straighten out the ones likely to be seen in your area. Even after that, though, there'll always be a slight problem distinguishing the Cooper's from one other accipiter, the sharp-shinned hawk, a close cousin (not included here as they migrate South in summer, but are as common as the Cooper's in winter).

The little sharpy looks very much like the Cooper's. The Cooper's is larger and has a more rounded tail.

The Cooper's hawk is a bird of woods and streamside groves. It lives by eating mostly other birds (as does the sharpy), which it surprises with swift pursuit in the close confines of the trees. Like other hawks of its genus, it seldom soars, preferring to flap and glide. It nests in conifers.

Our bird lives year-round over the entire United States, though, being not too common and in decline, it is infrequently seen these days. It might appear in a suburban backyard only fleetingly, though if it finds unwary birds at a feeder it may hang around for awhile.

Photos: (Above, right) Note the adult's bluish-gray back (from which it receives the local name "blue darter") and rounded, banded tail with white border. Bird at left shows horizontal breast banding and rounded end for the long tail. (Below) Back of a female shows more brown color, but long, striped tail and breast banding are still prominent.

The red-shouldered hawk is a "buteo": soaring hawks with short wings and stout bodies. This buteo, however, has longish wings and longish tail for its group. It flies somewhat like an accipiter, with flaps and glides, though it may also soar like a red-tailed hawk. But just let it open its mouth one time, and you know instantly what it is. "Kee-yar, kee-yar," or "kyear, kyear, kyear," it cries. Unlike the raspy whistle of its cousin the red-tail, the call of this hawk is one you can hear for miles. Blue jays frequently imitate it, but you wouldn't really be fooled. The hawk's cry is louder and stronger than theirs, as well as harsher and more fearsome.

Perched, the mature bird will show you a reddish belly or a back with red-brown shoulder patches. In flight, the black tail barred with white is a dead giveaway. Look also for a "translucent window" near the base of the primaries.

Whereas the red-tail can be found just about anywhere, the red-shouldered prefers to keep to streams, swamps, and moist woods. Its diet is mainly aquatic: frogs, turtles, snakes, though varied at times with rodents, rabbits, robins, screech owls, crows, wasps, and grasshoppers. Although colloquially termed "hen hawk," it seldom takes poultry.

Red-shouldered hawks stay paired for long periods, possibly for life. The record mating is 26 years. One book says they often return to the same nesting site season after season; another says they vary it. The nest is built of twigs, bark, leaves, and softer things, and is generally like that of the red-tailed hawk, only smaller.

Photos: The reddish breast and shoulder, along with the horizontal barring of the adult, are shown in both views. The black-and-white barred tail is better seen in the inset.

The mallard is one of our most common ducks, and certainly the one most people can name. It thrives in city and farm ponds. Sometimes it stays around because its wings have been clipped, but mostly because it knows where free food is!

With ducks, male and female are known as "drake" and "hen." Hens are usually a drab brown, hard to distinguish from hens of other species without study and field experience. The drakes of all our species have distinctive plumage and often a telltale body shape or habit of flight. After mating season, the drake goes into "eclipse" plumage, a duller garb than that which has recently attracted females.

Ducks can usefully be divided into several groups. The mallard is a "dabbler" or "puddle duck," meaning that it feeds on a shallow bottom by tipping its rear end skyward. It may also walk and feed on land. The pochards, or "diving ducks," have legs set far back to help them swim and feed under water, though this makes it awkward for them to walk on land.

The mallard drake is easily recognized: large yellow bill, green head with a white ring beneath. You may also spot its recurved tail, from which we get the term "duck-tail" (as in haircuts). With the hen, look for a brownish bird with an orange bill marked with black, a dark eye-stripe, and a blue wing-patch. That patch "the 'speculum'" is present in both sexes but not always visible.

The mallard offers an example of how bird watching and conservation go together. Most of our ducks require freshwater ponds and wetlands for their survival. In this century we have converted much wetland acreage into land for agriculture and living space. Such a practice, if continued, could lower the populations of ducks and other birds, taking some to extinction. For this reason many birders become avid conservationists, supporting public policies that protect habitat for wildlife.

Photos: Drake (above): yellow bill, green head, white neck stripe (and you can just make out the black feathers of the curled tail). Hen (middle): orange bill with dark top, dark eye-stripe. Her blue speculum shows clearly; the male's is hidden.

AMERICAN CROW
Corvus brachyrhynchos
17"

When crows wheel and circle overhead, you can admire their flight. And they're smarter than many birds: they can count as high as three or four. They're notoriously wary. They have many ways of making a living. Omnivorous, they'll eat grain, carrion, or whatever opportunity presents (peanuts in your backyard, eggs in a nest). This bodes well for this adaptable species.

 Crows are solid black with big thick bills. They're two or three times as large as any grackle or blackbird you'll see, but much smaller than the vultures that soar in the sky, and smaller than the ravens that inhabit our remote mountains. Their size varies substantially.

The only other bird you could normally confuse our American crow with is the fish crow, which lives mainly on the coast, although it has recently appeared around Atlanta in small numbers. Go by sound. The common crow says "caw, caw" or "awk awk awk awk." The fish crow has a very nasal cry, "car-ar." Alas, the summer juveniles of common crows can sound a lot like that! But if your bird says, "caw," then for sure it's an American Crow.

Crows roost and nest in rookeries, usually in isolated places. Abandoned crows' nests (stick platforms with deep centers) are sometimes used later by great horned owls and red-tailed hawks.

Crows don't know it, but they help bird watchers by pointing out the owls and hawks. They gather in numbers (5 to 25) to "mob" a predator. They carry on for ten or fifteen minutes, cawing harshly and stridently, and making passes at the owl. Keep your ears cocked for a mobbing, and you'll find owls and hawks.

Crows sometimes gather in flocks of hundreds, but it's more common to see them in groups of four or five. As they string out across the sky, they'll keep intervals of fifty to a hundred feet. When you drive along the interstate you can often recognize them just by this spacing.

If you're new at birding you may sometimes confuse a crow with a hawk. But crows are solid black, their beaks are straight and not hooked, and they tend to sit on the very tops of trees instead of a little way down.

Photos: No other solid black bird in our area is as large as the crow and has an eye as dark as its body.

The barred owl is a large owl, but slightly smaller than the great horned. It haunts swamps and bottoms, eating wetlands food. In size and habitat it stands to the great horned owl as the red-shouldered hawk does to the red-tailed.

From the front, observe the strong vertical dark-and-white barring (hence the name) on the breast. See the round head (no "horns") and the black (not yellow) eyes.

The most exciting thing about the barred owl is its song. Known familiarly as the "eight-hooter", it is often thought to say "Who cooks for you, who cooks for you-all?" But our owl has many variations on this basic song -- all of them rather loud. It may sing just the first half of its song, or it may add or subtract a note along the way. Often it gives a single long, descending, guttural howl: "hoo-aww". When it sings in duet with its mate, it barks and caws. Owl-prowlers sometimes ask: Was that an owl or a dog? By contrast, the great horned owl's song is soft, consisting of three notes plus two notes.

The barred owl nests in old hawk nests or hollow trees, but it will also use a properly-designed box. Breeding and nesting begin in late fall or early winter, enabling the young to have a long growing season.

The barred owl hunts actively in early morning, and even in mid-day. It may allow fairly close human approach, and can be lured into view by the proper calls (usually taped).

Photos: (Above) Note the dark brown vertical barring on the breast. Dark eyes and lack of "horns" easily distinguish the barred owl from the great horned. (Below) See how the owl's head is turned around backwards on its brown and white back.

RED-TAILED HAWK
Buteo jamaicensis
18"

The red-tailed hawk is common and widespread over the whole United States, soaring and hunting widely in open country. This buteo is quite successful as a bird of prey, being found in good numbers and having many subspecies. As long as humans don't poison the rodents it eats, this hawk will get along just fine.

You may see the red-tail perched along the interstate, white breast shining in the sun. Or you may see it gliding into the grass of the median for a kill. It is dark brown above with white underparts and usually a dark brown breast-band. Both sexes have the reddish tail. The immature, however, has a drab tail banded dark and light with gray or brown. The hawk's call is a rasping, one-note whistle that sounds almost like steam escaping.

This hawk finds a tall tree in which to build a flat nest of twigs and sticks over two feet in diameter. It brings new green sprigs as long as the eggs are incubating. During this time the male also brings food to his mate. Nests may be re-used.

In the beginning it will take some care to tell a soaring red-tail from a vulture. They're about the same size and soar in the same way, sometimes even together. But a vulture is definitely black, whereas a red-tail will appear brown. The turkey vulture holds its wings in a vee (dihedral), whereas the hawk holds its flat. If you can view the undertail against the sunlight, you'll see the reddish of the feathers showing through with a faint pink: definite ID.

Our hawk may hunt from perches near open fields or from the air. It may perch high -- two thirds of the way up a tree -- or low as a fence post. It wants small rodents: rats, mice, rabbits, squirrels. It will take snakes, it will take road-kill. On rare occasions it takes a bird. Chickens? No, this is not a chicken hawk. Help discourage farmers from shooting this beneficial bird: it eats the rats and squirrels that steal his corn!

Photos: (Above) The undertail is only faintly washed with red. Note the dark hooded head. This bird has a dark breast band, usually a reliable field mark. (Middle inset) Our hawk's tail color is about that of a robin's breast. (Below) Immature birds have stripes on their tails, as are barely visible here. In all three pictures, note the buteo traits: heavy body and short tail.

GREAT HORNED OWL
Bubo virginianus
20"

The great horned owl generally calls with five soft hoots: "hoo-huh-hoooo, hoo-hoo". At night you can easily tell it apart from any other owl by this song alone. This is the largest owl in our area. It uses its wickedly sharp talons to capture anything that moves from dusk to dawn: squirrel, skunk, bird, rat, snake. As with many birds of prey, the female is larger than the male. Her size gives her a little more control and protection during the mating process, and makes her a proficient hunter of larger prey.

The great horned roosts by day in deep shade, where it is often harder to see than you might expect, considering its size. Its hiding place is sometimes disclosed by the mobbing of crows, whose frenzied chorus of caws alerts the observer to its presence.

Great horned owls mate in mid-winter and nest very early, often occupying an abandoned crow or hawk nest. The chicks, one or two, will be out during early spring. These birds get such an early start because they need a long season to grow before they're ready to survive the coming winter on their own. The chicks are fuzzy gray and surprisingly large. Their food-begging call, given about every half-minute, is a loud, rasping "screep".

The bird is named for its horns, which are nothing more than tufts of feathers. Look for yellow eyes (the non-horned barred owl has black eyes). A large, white bib under the throat will be prominently visible. The light breast is barred with horizontal striping (vertical for the barred). The back is mottled brown and gray. There are twelve subspecies north of Mexico, each with its own slight color variations.

The great horned owl manages to survive in the metro area perhaps because so many large city trees escape the logger's saw, and because we have so many squirrels and other small mammals. One expert estimates that there could be as many as fifty pairs inside the perimeter.

Photos: "Horns" may be relaxed and flapping to the side, or sticking up as if to make the bird look fiercer. Note yellow eyes (black pupil), white bib, horizontal barring on breast. The reddish-brown facial disk is also worth observing. And get a look at those claws!

BLACK VULTURE	**TURKEY VULTURE**
Coragyps atratus	*Cathartes aura*
22"	25"

Turkey vultures and black vultures often soar and feed together, though usually turkey vultures are more prevalent. If you're watching a group of vultures, inspect each one to see exactly what you have.

The black vulture (left) has an all-gray head, not the blood-red head of the turkey vulture. It has white feathers only on the tips of its wings while the turkey vulture has white from the wingtips to the body along the trailing edge. These are marks you can note easily within several hundred yards.

Farther away, notice that the black vulture flies with its wings straight out. The turkey vulture (below), on the other hand, has a pronounced "V" shape where the wings meet the body when viewed from the front or back (not shown). This v-shape can be seen from miles away as the TV soars through the skies looking for a meal and also distinguishes it from the hawks, usually the red-tailed hawk, that also soar around the Georgia skies.

Note further that the tail of the black vulture is extremely short, so that wings and tail seem to blend into one. Some call the black vulture "short-tail."

Both species nest right on the ground in some dark, secluded spot and feast on carrion, i.e., we see both species tugging at road kills beside the interstate highways. Turkey vultures have a good sense of smell and locate the food before black vultures.

They rarely vocalize so you cannot distinguish them by ear.

Photos: The turkey vulture (above) shows reddish head and the entire rear half of the wing is white, as is the tip. With the black vulture (below), only the tips of the wings are white and the head is gray. The former characteristic is an excellent field mark when vultures are soaring.

What is the big brown and black goose grazing or preening so serenely at the edges of our city and county lakes? The Canada goose. In recent years these stately birds, forsaking their migratory nature when brought here, have taken up permanent residence in Metro ponds and lakes. Some consider them a great nuisance; and such, indeed, they may have become.

There is no mistaking the bird. No other goose has the long black neck with the stark white under-chin. No other is so loved by bread-throwers at city ponds and parks, or so hated by lakeside home owners who must deal with their excrement. On the other hand, they're said to be quite tasty.

Canada geese mate for life. They are smart, strong, and protective of their young. As with bears: do not come between the mother and her young. An enraged goose is a fearsome bird.

The call of the migrating Canada goose is described as "ka-runk, ha-lunk," or "honk-a-lonk". The V-formation passes overhead between north and south. Bird watchers should be aware, however, that the migrant most often seen and heard over the Atlanta area is not the Canada goose but the sandhill crane (not shown). The latter has a gurgling trill, not a honk. Sandhills regularly fly over Atlanta on route between their wintering grounds in the Okefenokee Swamp and their breeding grounds in the Northwest. Let "sandhill crane" be your first thought when you catch sight of a large V of migrating birds.

As with the great horned owl, song sparrow, and many other species, the Canada goose is divided by ornithologists into subspecies, each with its own distinctive characteristics. Size, breast color, ring on neck, all bespeak variations in the inherited genome. Wild populations differ greatly. How else would they ever have evolved into the multifarious forms we see around us?

Photos: Can't mistake this bird for any other with its black neck and head, white chinstrap and cheek. The upper side is generally described as brownish gray.

The great blue heron is Atlanta's largest water bird. It has a six-foot wingspan and stands three feet tall. It is steely blue-gray, with a black patch on the shoulder. It is often seen standing at the edge of pond or stream with its long neck either straight or curved into a beautiful S above its shoulders. It flies with deep slow strokes, legs extended, and neck folded into a tight curve. Cranes and geese fly with their necks straight out.

This bird could be confused with the yellow-crowned night heron, which is smaller, shorter, and less common. The night heron has a short black bill, whereas our great blue heron has a long yellow one. If you are seeing it from a good distance, the only other possible bird you might think it resemble would be a wood stork which has a similar size, but its colors are black and white rather than the blues and grays of the great blue, and the wood stork's bill is very large and curved.

Ranging widely over most of the United States, the great blue feeds by spearing fish with its bill, tossing them in the air, and catching them head-first for swallowing. Occasionally it stakes out backyard fishponds, going for a gourmet meal of koi or goldfish. When alarmed, it flies off with a harsh grunt; otherwise it is silent. Look for them along the banks of the rivers, in ponds of all sizes, and along marsh edges.

The great blue heron builds a nest of sticks in a wetland setting. In the last century and the early part of this one, the feathers of herons and egrets were prized for ladies' hats, resulting in extensive hunting and population decline, as mentioned for several other species in this book.

Photos: The curled neck position is assumed during flight and preparatory to spearing fish (upper photo). The water's edge shown here (below) is typical of what this heron likes. With its neck extended, the great blue heron's height of over three feet gives it an excellent view of fish. The bird's size makes it unmistakable even from a distance, and check that dagger-like beak!

ABOUT THE AUTHORS

Jim Wilson is from Pensacola, Florida, and received his B.S. in Physics from the University of Florida. After four years as a naval aviator, he went on to obtain an M.S. in Radiation Biophysics (UF), and then a Ph.D. in Neurophysiology from the University of Virginia. He was a researcher and teacher at Emory University before taking an early retirement to pursue bird activities. He served on the Board of Directors of the Atlanta Audubon Society for eight years, including President, and became the first staff person for this society as the Important Bird Areas Program Coordinator.

Anselm Atkins, from Texas, was a monk-priest for fifteen years at the Trappist monastery in Conyers. He obtained his doctorate in "Literature and Theology" from Emory University in 1971. His publications ranged from this subject area to art, ornithology, and natural history. He edited the Atlanta Audubon Society's newsletter, *Wingbars*, for sixteen years. His novel *The Notebooks of Lana Skimnest* is about a nature-loving woman. The computer graphics in the present text reflect his interest in art, as did his colored glass works. He died in 1999.